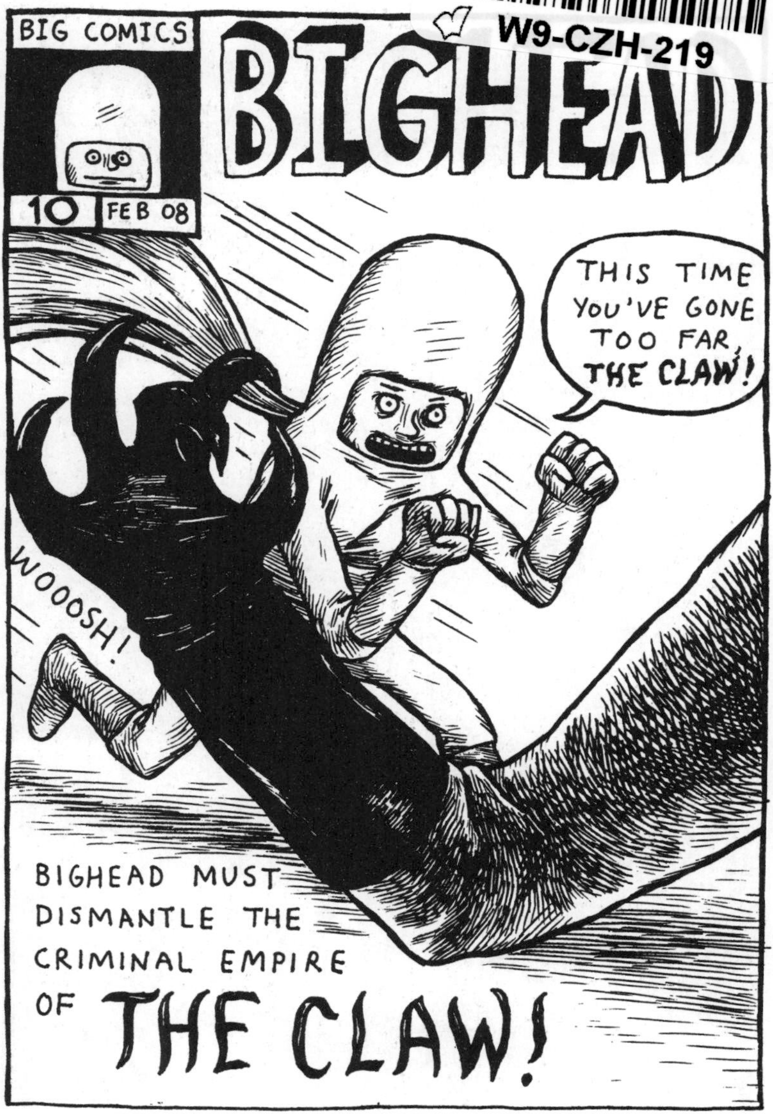
BIG COMICS
BIGHEAD
10
FEB 08
THIS TIME YOU'VE GONE TOO FAR, THE CLAW!
WOOOSH!
BIGHEAD MUST DISMANTLE THE CRIMINAL EMPIRE OF THE CLAW!

BIGHEAD SITS AT HOME, QUIETLY RELAXING

SUDDENLY...

WHAT--WHAT'S HAP--HAPPENING?! I BETTER FIND OUT!

RUMMMBBBBBBBBLLE!

ENTERTAINMENT NEWS... BASEBALL SCORES... HOUSE FIXING REALITY SHOW... AH, HERE WE GO!

CLICK
CLICK
CLICK
CLICK

..THAT'S RIGHT, SUE. AND AMAZINGLY ENOUGH, THE EARTHQUAKE WE JUST HAD REGISTERED 3.1415929 ON THE RICHTER SCALE - OR PI!

...BREAKING NEWS...BREAKI

COINCIDENCE? NOT ACCORDING TO LOCAL SUPERVILLAIN, CLAW.

THE CLAW.

THIS EARTHQUAKE IS A DISPLAY OF MY POWER. YOUR CITY WILL DELIVER 300 MILLION DOLLARS TO ME -- OR ELSE!

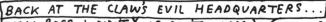

BACK AT THE CLAW'S EVIL HEADQUARTERS...

WOW, BOSS, I DIDNT KNOW WE HAD THE POWER TO MAKE EARTHQUAKES

WE DON'T. I WAS JUST TAKING CREDIT TO MAKE US LOOK MORE BAD-ASS.

BUT WE'RE ALL MILLIONAIRES ALREADY. WHY ARE WE ASKING FOR MONEY?

HACK

SLASH

NOW... DOES ANYONE ELSE HAVE ANY QUESTIONS?

YES, NIGHT MINISTER.

MAYBE WE SHOULD USE OUR POWER TO IMPOSE OUR POLITICAL WILL.

THAT'S NOT A QUESTION.

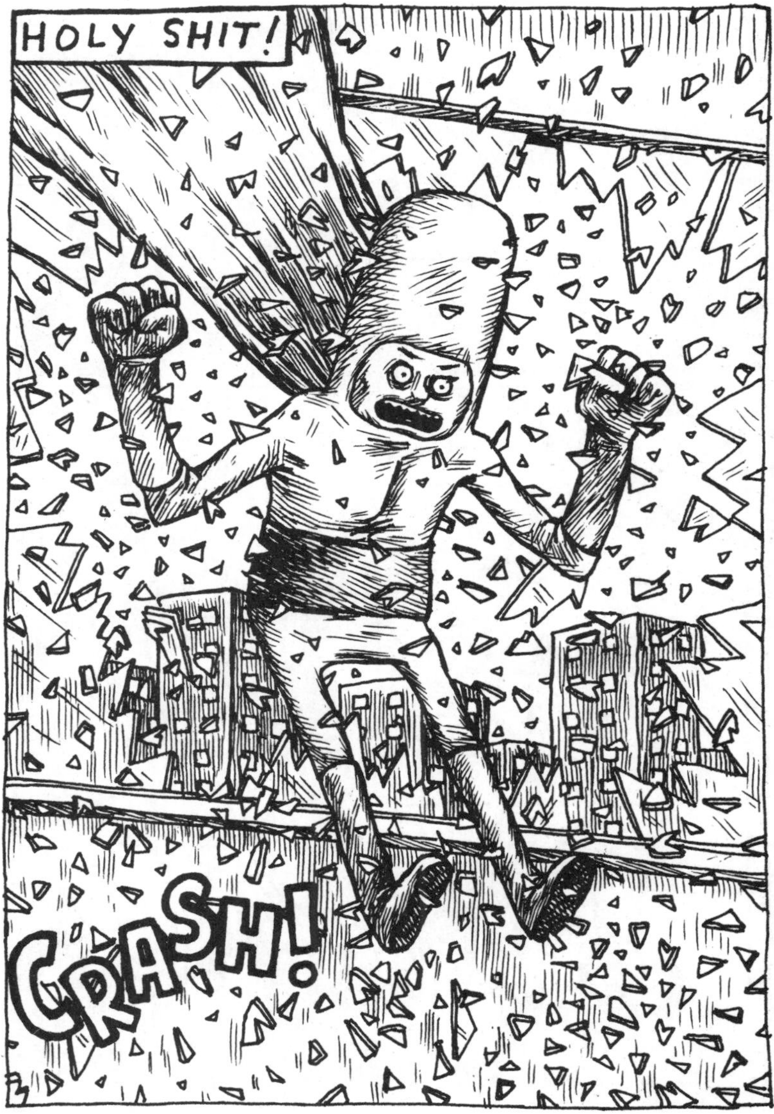
HOLY SHIT!
CRASH!

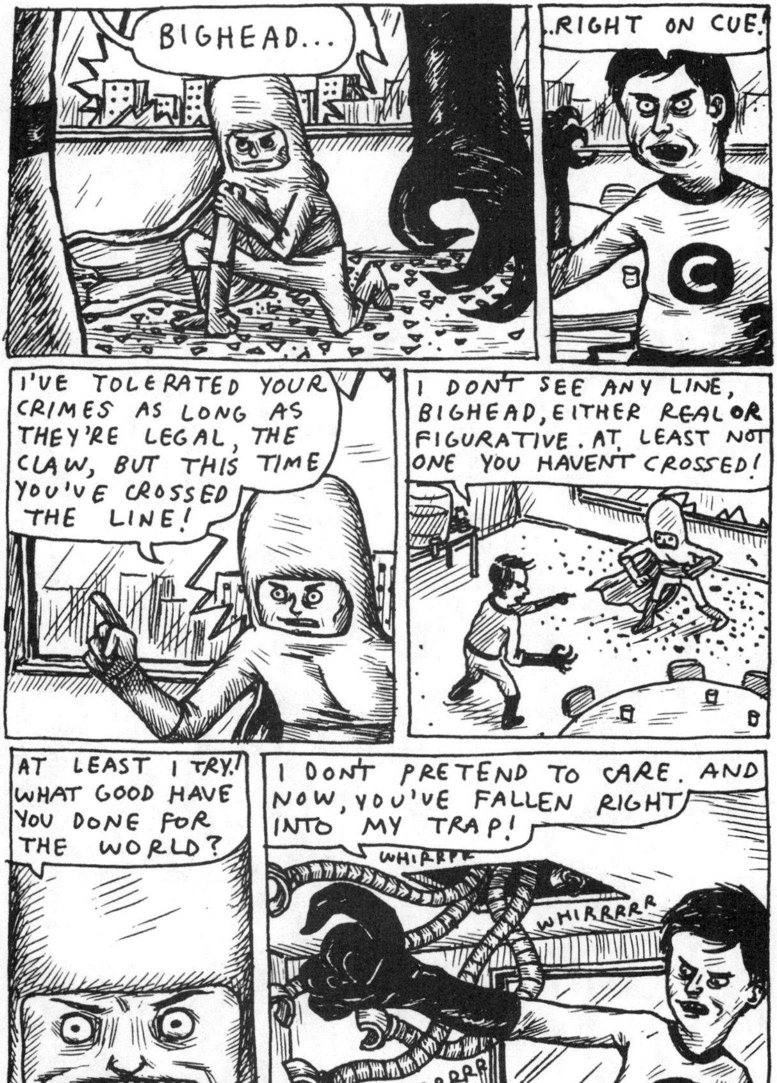
BIGHEAD...
..RIGHT ON CUE!
I'VE TOLERATED YOUR CRIMES AS LONG AS THEY'RE LEGAL, THE CLAW, BUT THIS TIME YOU'VE CROSSED THE LINE!
I DONT SEE ANY LINE, BIGHEAD, EITHER REAL OR FIGURATIVE. AT LEAST NOT ONE YOU HAVENT CROSSED!
AT LEAST I TRY! WHAT GOOD HAVE YOU DONE FOR THE WORLD?
I DONT PRETEND TO CARE. AND NOW, YOU'VE FALLEN RIGHT INTO MY TRAP!
WHIRRRR
WHIRRRRR
WHIRRRRR

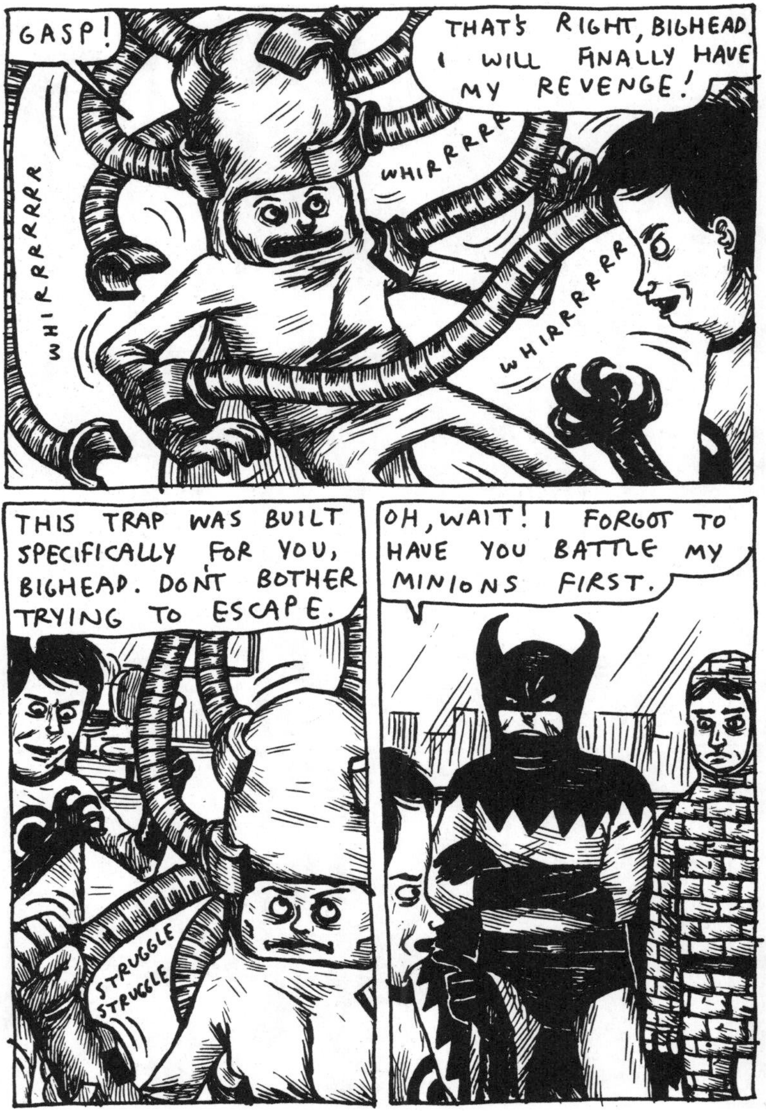
GASP!
THAT'S RIGHT, BIGHEAD. I WILL FINALLY HAVE MY REVENGE!
WHIRRRRRR
WHIRRRRR
WHIRRRRRR
THIS TRAP WAS BUILT SPECIFICALLY FOR YOU, BIGHEAD. DON'T BOTHER TRYING TO ESCAPE.
STRUGGLE STRUGGLE
OH, WAIT! I FORGOT TO HAVE YOU BATTLE MY MINIONS FIRST.

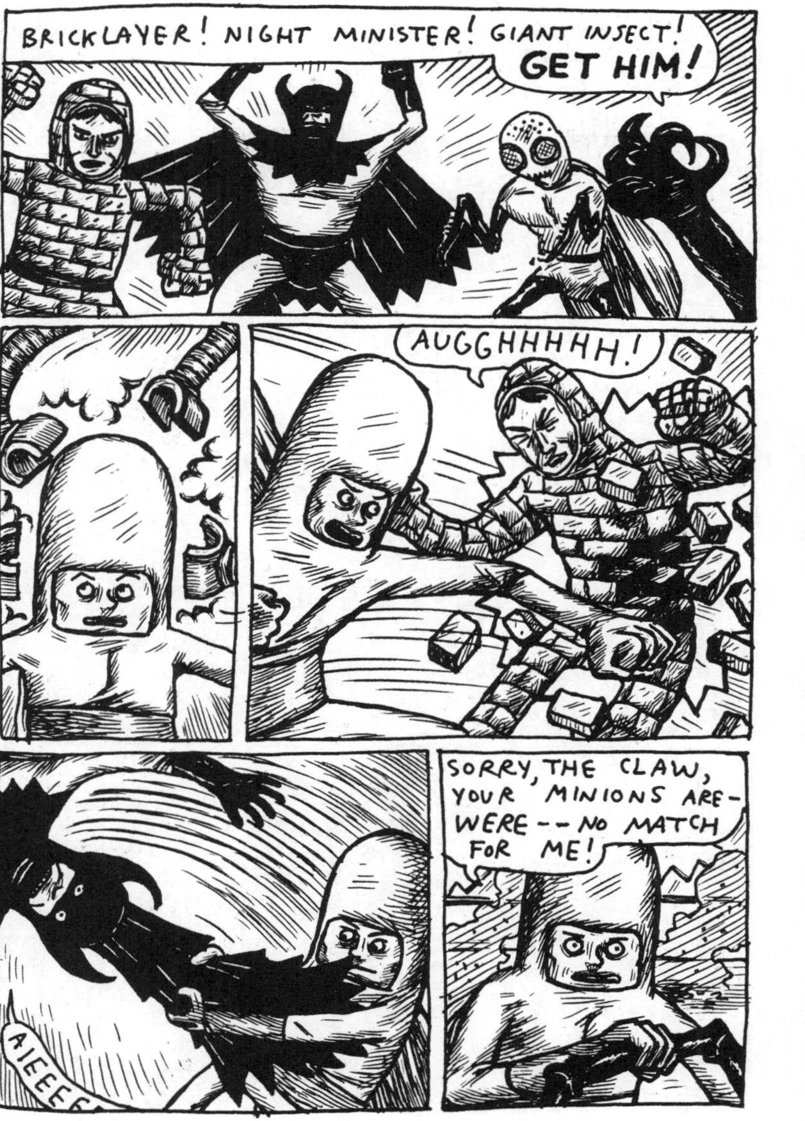
BRICKLAYER! NIGHT MINISTER! GIANT INSECT!
GET HIM!
AUGGHHHHH!
AIEEEE
SORRY, THE CLAW, YOUR MINIONS ARE- WERE -- NO MATCH FOR ME!

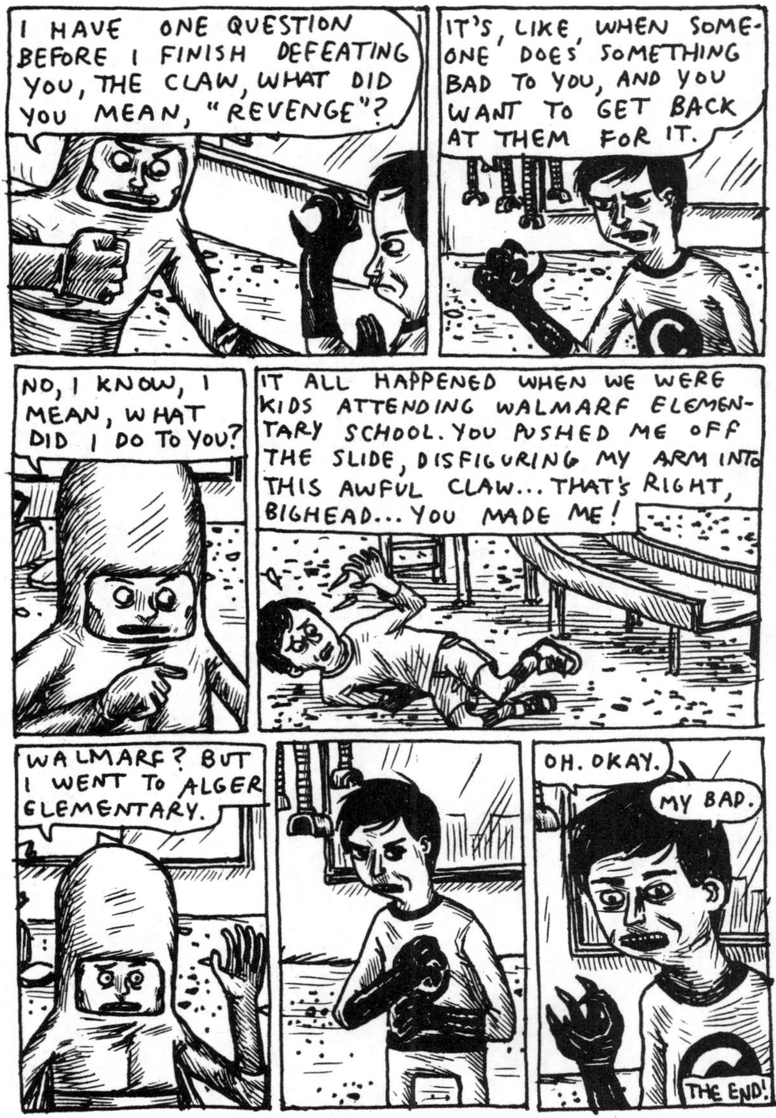
I HAVE ONE QUESTION BEFORE I FINISH DEFEATING YOU, THE CLAW, WHAT DID YOU MEAN, "REVENGE"?
IT'S, LIKE, WHEN SOMEONE DOES SOMETHING BAD TO YOU, AND YOU WANT TO GET BACK AT THEM FOR IT.
NO, I KNOW, I MEAN, WHAT DID I DO TO YOU?
IT ALL HAPPENED WHEN WE WERE KIDS ATTENDING WALMARF ELEMENTARY SCHOOL. YOU PUSHED ME OFF THE SLIDE, DISFIGURING MY ARM INTO THIS AWFUL CLAW... THAT'S RIGHT, BIGHEAD... YOU MADE ME!
WALMARF? BUT I WENT TO ALGER ELEMENTARY.
OH. OKAY.
MY BAD.
THE END!

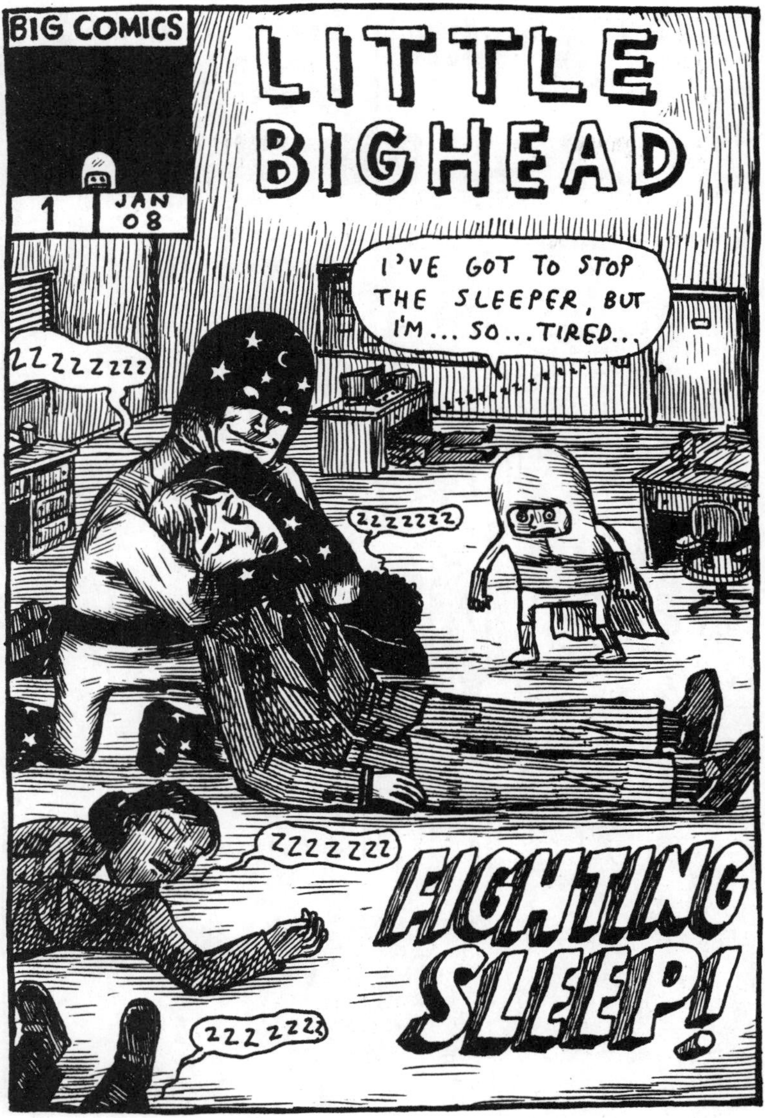
BIG COMICS
1
JAN 08
LITTLE BIGHEAD
I'VE GOT TO STOP THE SLEEPER, BUT I'M... SO... TIRED...
ZZZZZZZZZ
ZZZZZZZ
ZZZZZZZ
ZZZZZZZ
FIGHTING SLEEP!

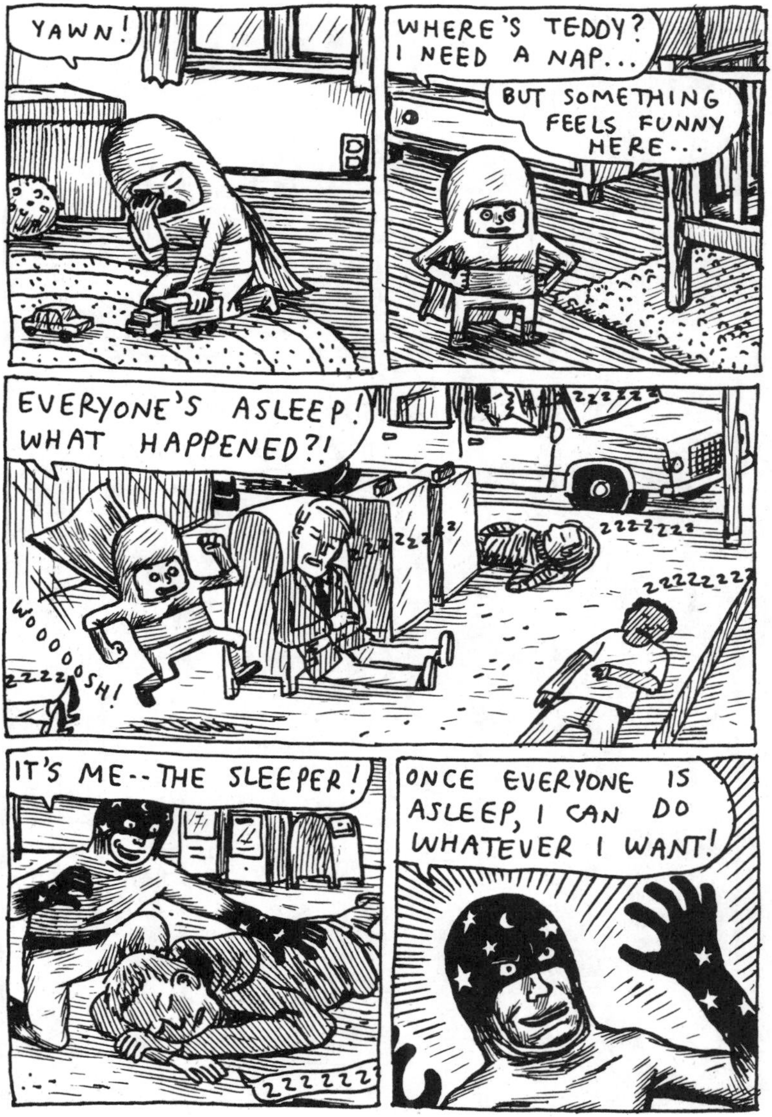
YAWN!
WHERE'S TEDDY? I NEED A NAP...
BUT SOMETHING FEELS FUNNY HERE...
EVERYONE'S ASLEEP! WHAT HAPPENED?!
WOOOOOOSH!
IT'S ME--THE SLEEPER!
ONCE EVERYONE IS ASLEEP, I CAN DO WHATEVER I WANT!

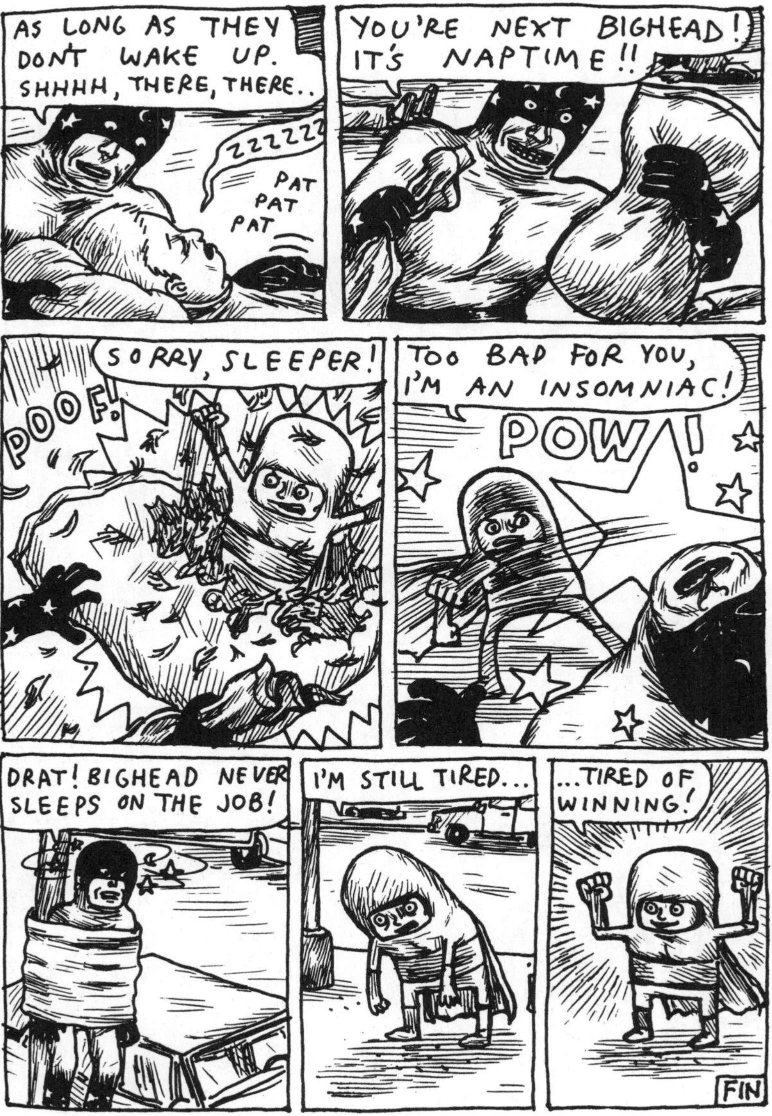
AS LONG AS THEY DON'T WAKE UP. SHHHH, THERE, THERE..
ZZZZZZ
PAT PAT PAT
YOU'RE NEXT BIGHEAD! IT'S NAPTIME!!
SORRY, SLEEPER!
POOF!
TOO BAD FOR YOU, I'M AN INSOMNIAC!
POW!
DRAT! BIGHEAD NEVER SLEEPS ON THE JOB!
I'M STILL TIRED...
...TIRED OF WINNING!
FIN

SOMETIMES I'M SAD
BY: THE SUPER INVISIBLE MAN

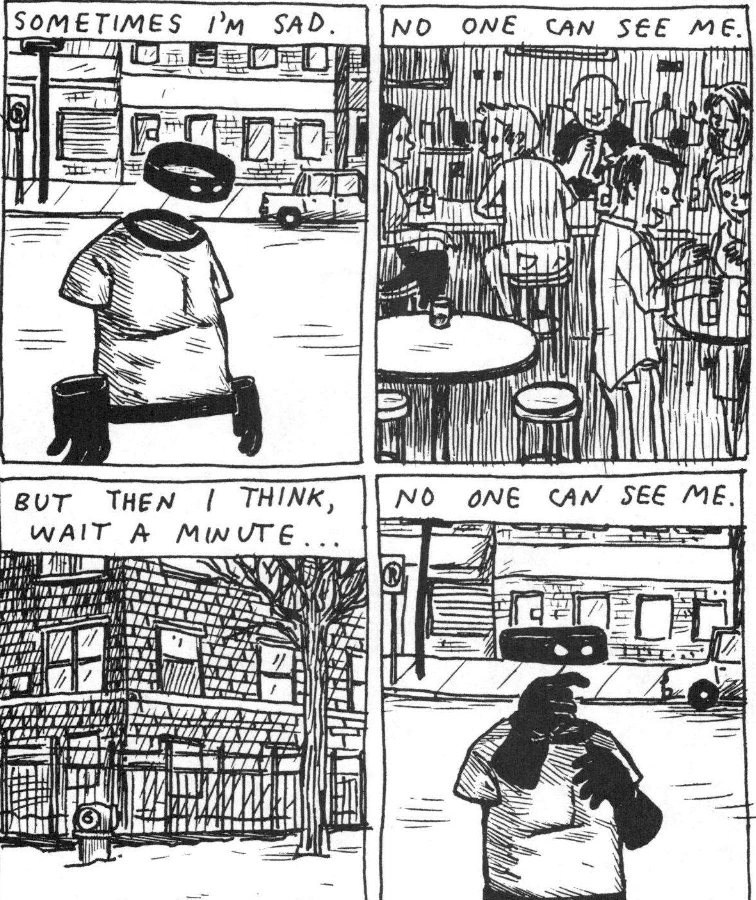
SOMETIMES I'M SAD.
NO ONE CAN SEE ME.
BUT THEN I THINK, WAIT A MINUTE...
NO ONE CAN SEE ME.

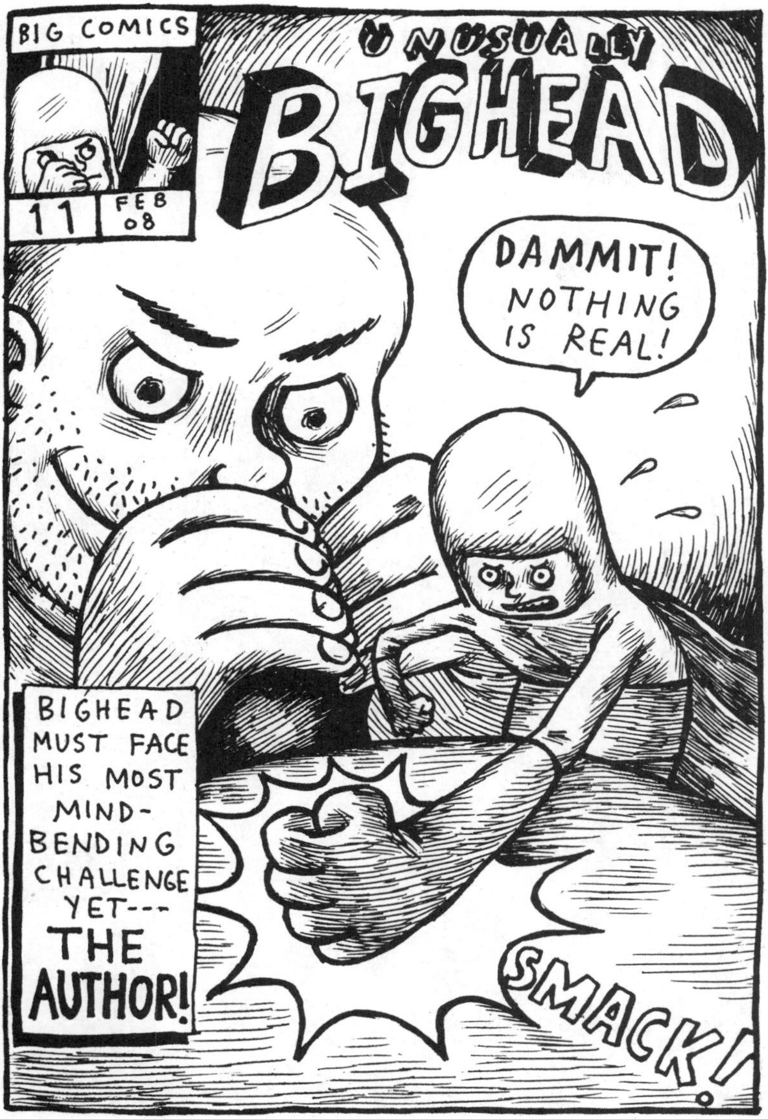
BIG COMICS
11
FEB 08
UNUSUALLY
BIGHEAD
DAMMIT! NOTHING IS REAL!
BIGHEAD MUST FACE HIS MOST MIND-BENDING CHALLENGE YET--- THE AUTHOR!
SMACK!

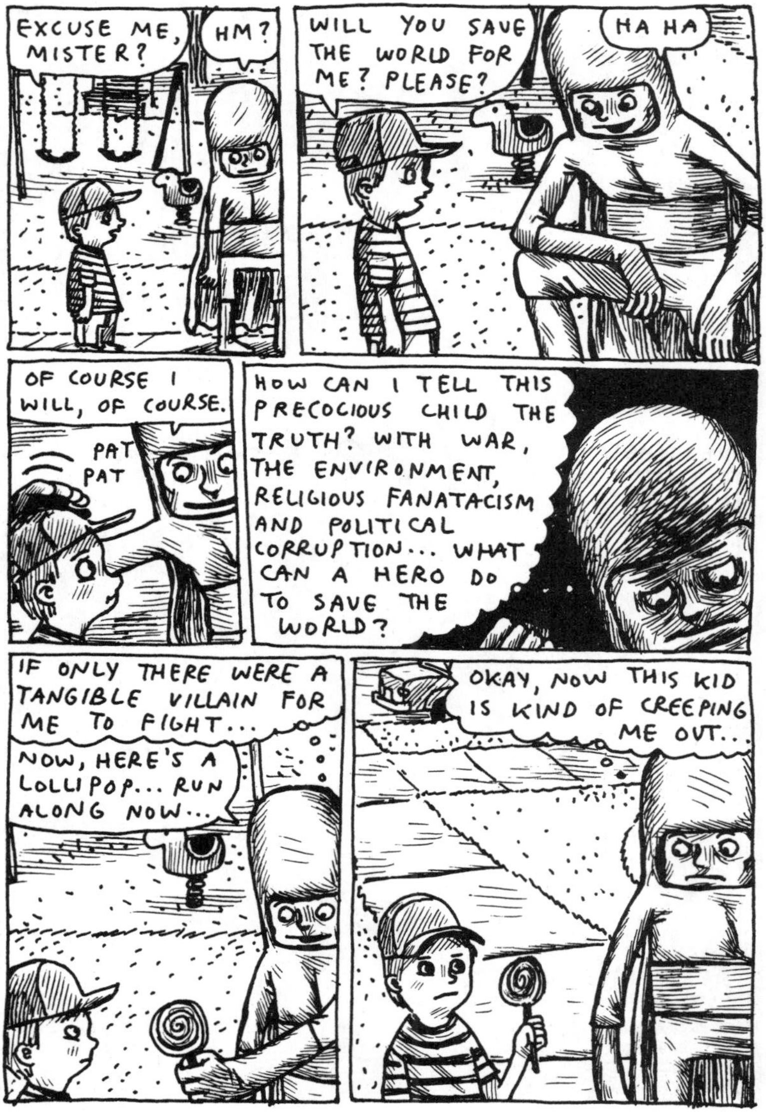
EXCUSE ME, MISTER?
HM?
WILL YOU SAVE THE WORLD FOR ME? PLEASE?
HA HA
OF COURSE I WILL, OF COURSE.
PAT PAT
HOW CAN I TELL THIS PRECOCIOUS CHILD THE TRUTH? WITH WAR, THE ENVIRONMENT, RELIGIOUS FANATACISM AND POLITICAL CORRUPTION... WHAT CAN A HERO DO TO SAVE THE WORLD?
IF ONLY THERE WERE A TANGIBLE VILLAIN FOR ME TO FIGHT...
NOW, HERE'S A LOLLIPOP... RUN ALONG NOW...
OKAY, NOW THIS KID IS KIND OF CREEPING ME OUT...

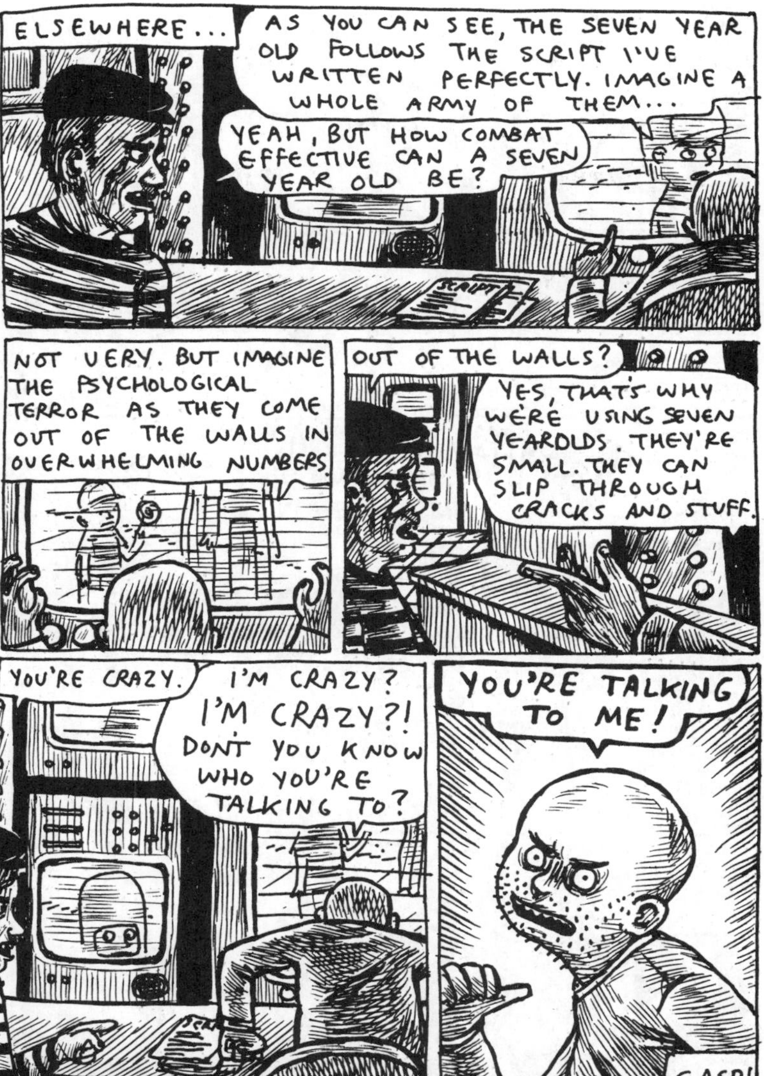
ELSEWHERE...
AS YOU CAN SEE, THE SEVEN YEAR OLD FOLLOWS THE SCRIPT I'VE WRITTEN PERFECTLY. IMAGINE A WHOLE ARMY OF THEM...
YEAH, BUT HOW COMBAT EFFECTIVE CAN A SEVEN YEAR OLD BE?
SCRIPT
NOT VERY. BUT IMAGINE THE PSYCHOLOGICAL TERROR AS THEY COME OUT OF THE WALLS IN OVERWHELMING NUMBERS.
OUT OF THE WALLS?
YES, THAT'S WHY WE'RE USING SEVEN YEAROLDS. THEY'RE SMALL. THEY CAN SLIP THROUGH CRACKS AND STUFF.
YOU'RE CRAZY.
I'M CRAZY? I'M CRAZY?! DON'T YOU KNOW WHO YOU'RE TALKING TO?
YOU'RE TALKING TO ME!
GASP!

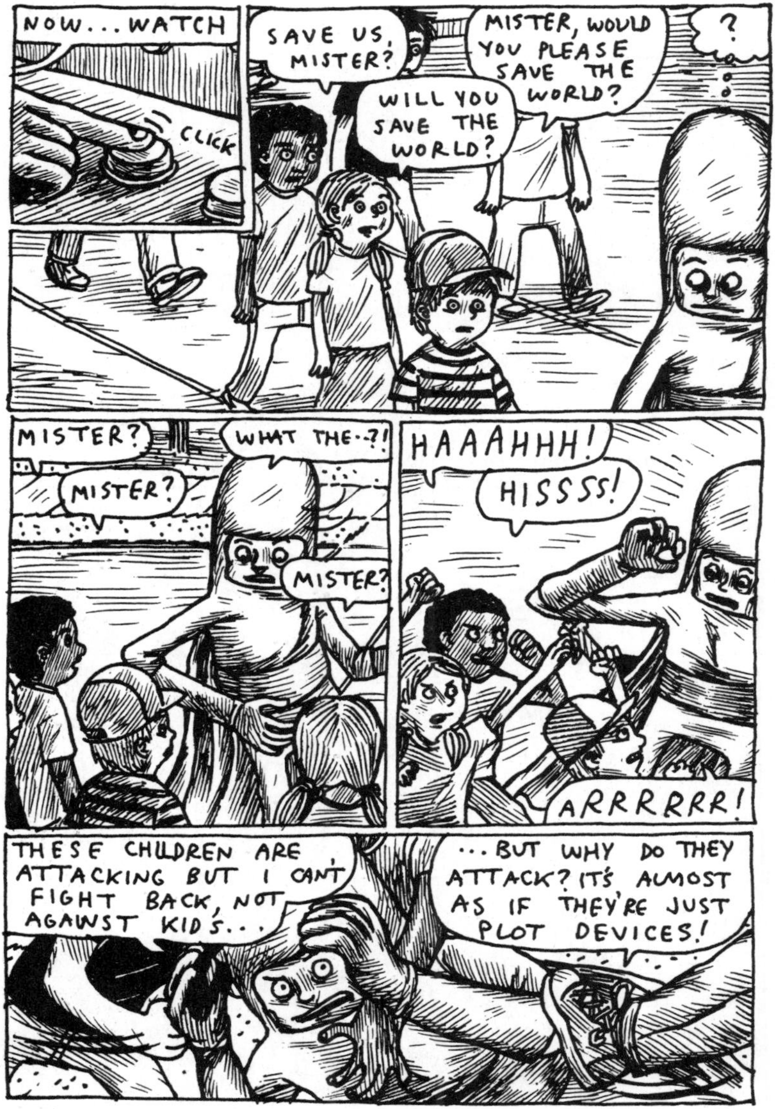
NOW...WATCH
CLICK
SAVE US, MISTER?
MISTER, WOULD YOU PLEASE SAVE THE WORLD?
?
WILL YOU SAVE THE WORLD?
MISTER?
WHAT THE--?!
MISTER?
MISTER?
HAAAHHH!
HISSSS!
ARRRRRRR!
THESE CHILDREN ARE ATTACKING BUT I CAN'T FIGHT BACK, NOT AGAINST KID'S...
...BUT WHY DO THEY ATTACK? IT'S ALMOST AS IF THEY'RE JUST PLOT DEVICES!

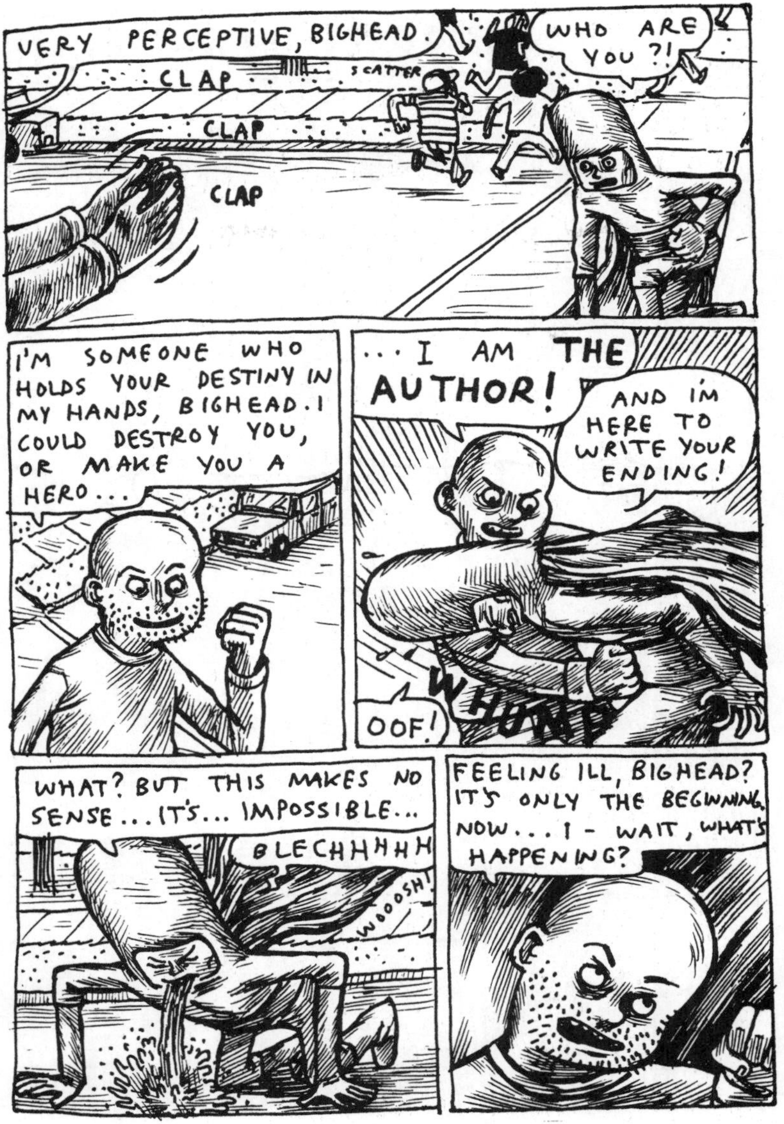
VERY PERCEPTIVE, BIGHEAD.
WHO ARE YOU ?!
CLAP
SCATTER
CLAP
CLAP
I'M SOMEONE WHO HOLDS YOUR DESTINY IN MY HANDS, BIGHEAD. I COULD DESTROY YOU, OR MAKE YOU A HERO...
... I AM THE AUTHOR!
AND I'M HERE TO WRITE YOUR ENDING!
WHUMP
OOF!
WHAT? BUT THIS MAKES NO SENSE... IT'S... IMPOSSIBLE...
BLECHHHHH
WOOOSH!
FEELING ILL, BIGHEAD? IT'S ONLY THE BEGINNING NOW... I - WAIT, WHAT'S HAPPENING?

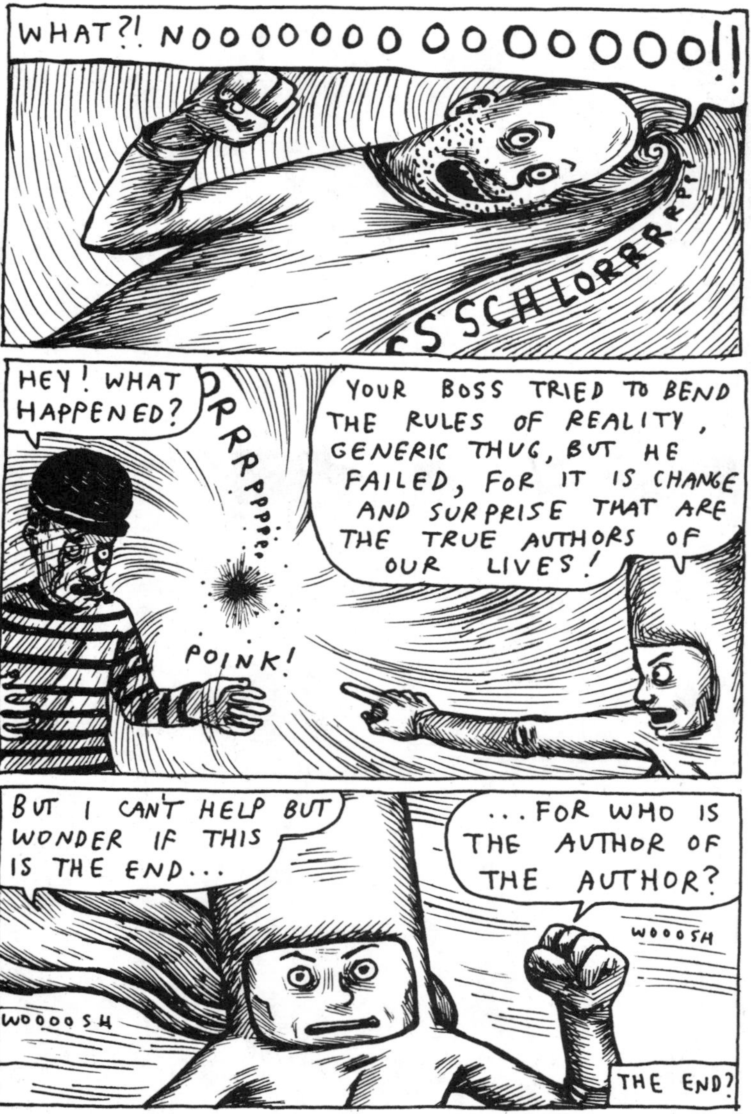
WHAT?! NOOOOOOOOOOOOOO!!
SSSCHLORRRRRRPP
HEY! WHAT HAPPENED?
RRRPPPPP
YOUR BOSS TRIED TO BEND THE RULES OF REALITY, GENERIC THUG, BUT HE FAILED, FOR IT IS CHANGE AND SURPRISE THAT ARE THE TRUE AUTHORS OF OUR LIVES!
POINK!
BUT I CAN'T HELP BUT WONDER IF THIS IS THE END...
...FOR WHO IS THE AUTHOR OF THE AUTHOR?
WOOOSH
WOOOOSH
THE END?

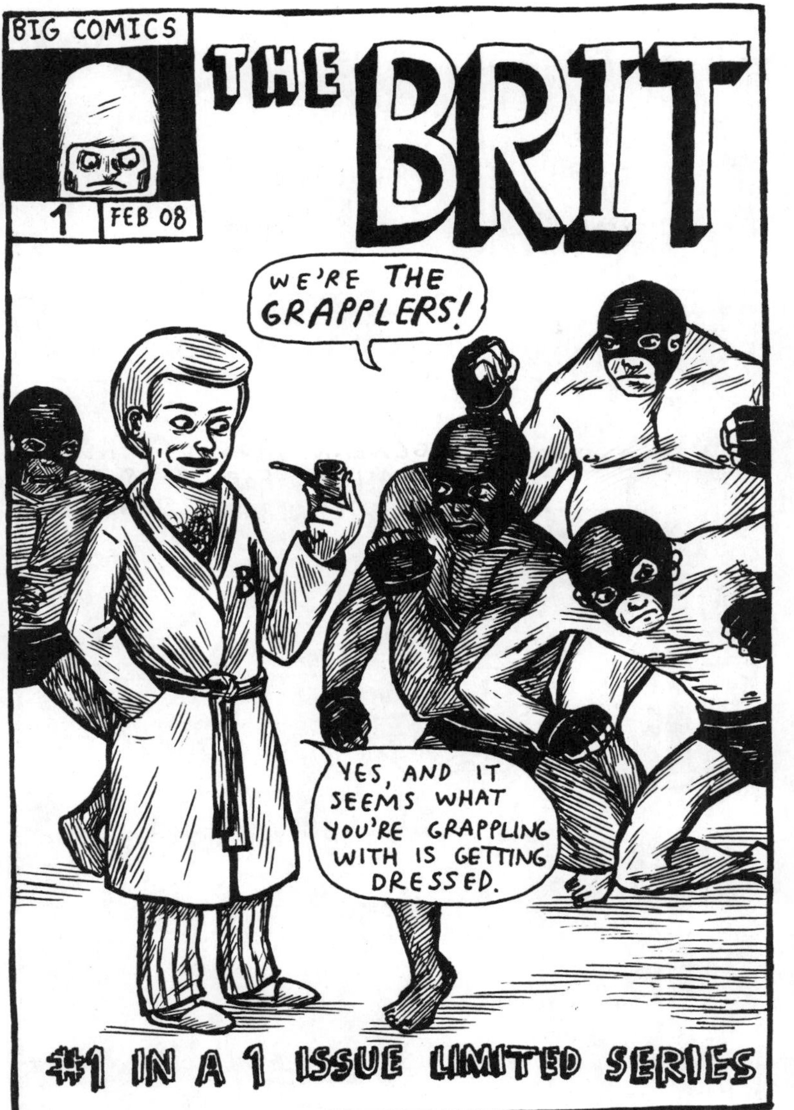
BIG COMICS
1
FEB 08
THE BRIT
WE'RE THE GRAPPLERS!
YES, AND IT SEEMS WHAT YOU'RE GRAPPLING WITH IS GETTING DRESSED.
#1 IN A 1 ISSUE LIMITED SERIES

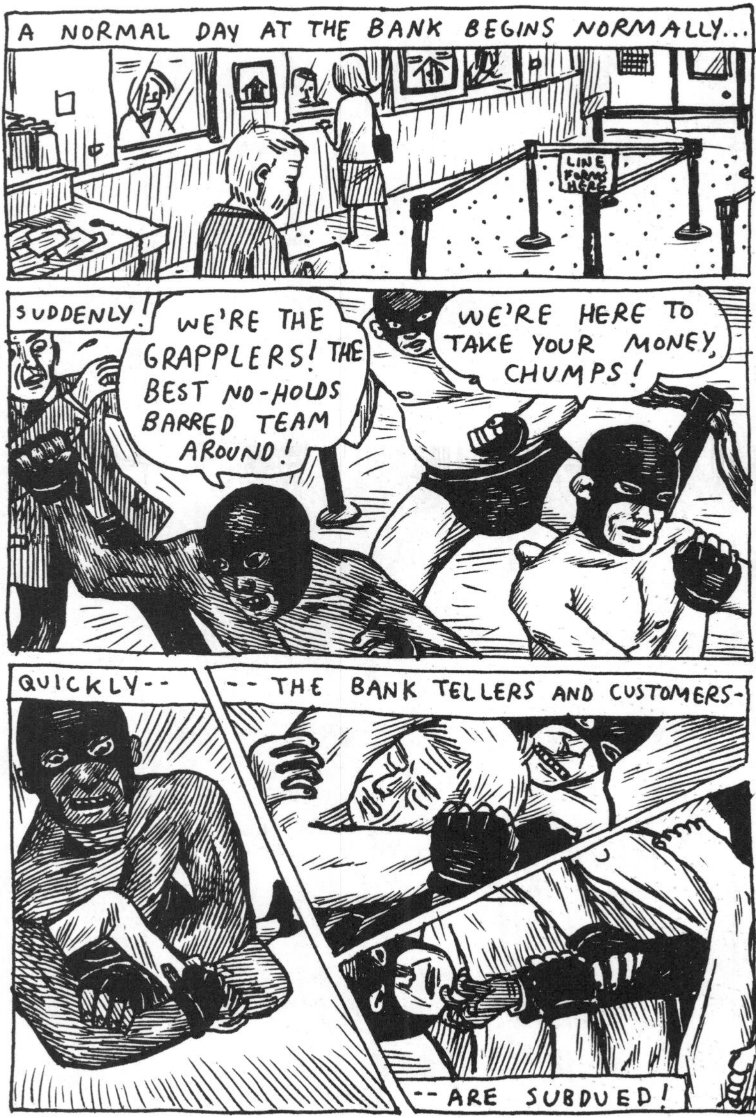
A NORMAL DAY AT THE BANK BEGINS NORMALLY...
LINE FORMS HERE
SUDDENLY!
WE'RE THE GRAPPLERS! THE BEST NO-HOLDS BARRED TEAM AROUND!
WE'RE HERE TO TAKE YOUR MONEY, CHUMPS!
QUICKLY--
-- THE BANK TELLERS AND CUSTOMERS-
--ARE SUBDUED!

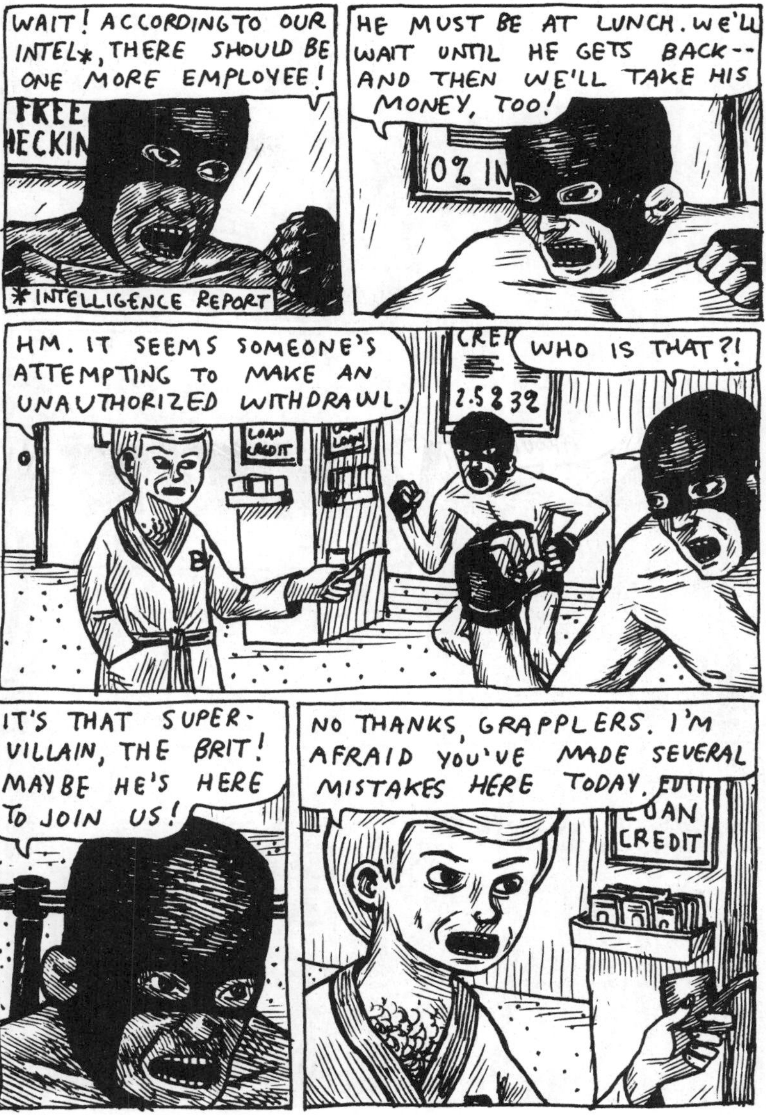
WAIT! ACCORDING TO OUR INTEL*, THERE SHOULD BE ONE MORE EMPLOYEE!
FREE
HECKIN
*INTELLIGENCE REPORT
HE MUST BE AT LUNCH. WE'LL WAIT UNTIL HE GETS BACK-- AND THEN WE'LL TAKE HIS MONEY, TOO!
0% IN
HM. IT SEEMS SOMEONE'S ATTEMPTING TO MAKE AN UNAUTHORIZED WITHDRAWL.
LOAN CREDIT
CRED
2.5232
WHO IS THAT?!
IT'S THAT SUPER-VILLAIN, THE BRIT! MAYBE HE'S HERE TO JOIN US!
NO THANKS, GRAPPLERS. I'M AFRAID YOU'VE MADE SEVERAL MISTAKES HERE TODAY.
LOAN CREDIT

UNBEKNOWNST TO THE GRAPPLERS, THE BRIT'S ALTER EGO STEPHEN HAS SPENT COUNTLESS HOURS WATCHING MIXED MARTIAL ARTS COMPETITIONS.

WE DON'T UNDERSTAND. YOU'RE A VILLAIN, LIKE US! WE'RE ON THE SAME SIDE!

AS I SAID, YOU'RE MISTAKEN, OLD CHAP. PEOPLE JUST THINK I'M A VILLAIN BECAUSE OF BIGHEAD... HE'S A BIT RESENTFUL OF ME BECAUSE I MARRIED THE LASS HE FANCIES, POOR BLOKE.

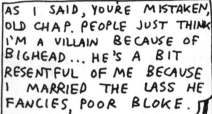

LATER...

YOU MISSED ALL THE EXCITEMENT, STEPHEN.

EXCITEMENT?! OH MY!

HA HA HA!

FIN

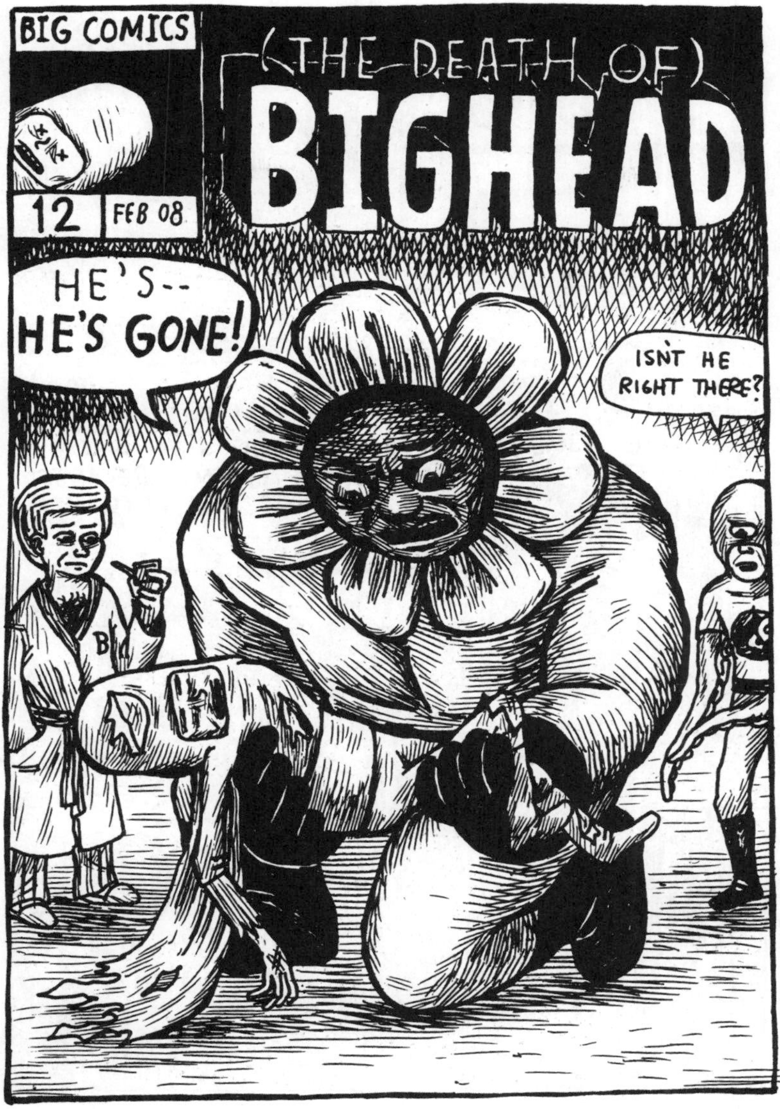
BIG COMICS
(THE DEATH OF)
BIGHEAD
12
FEB 08
HE'S-- HE'S GONE!
ISN'T HE RIGHT THERE?

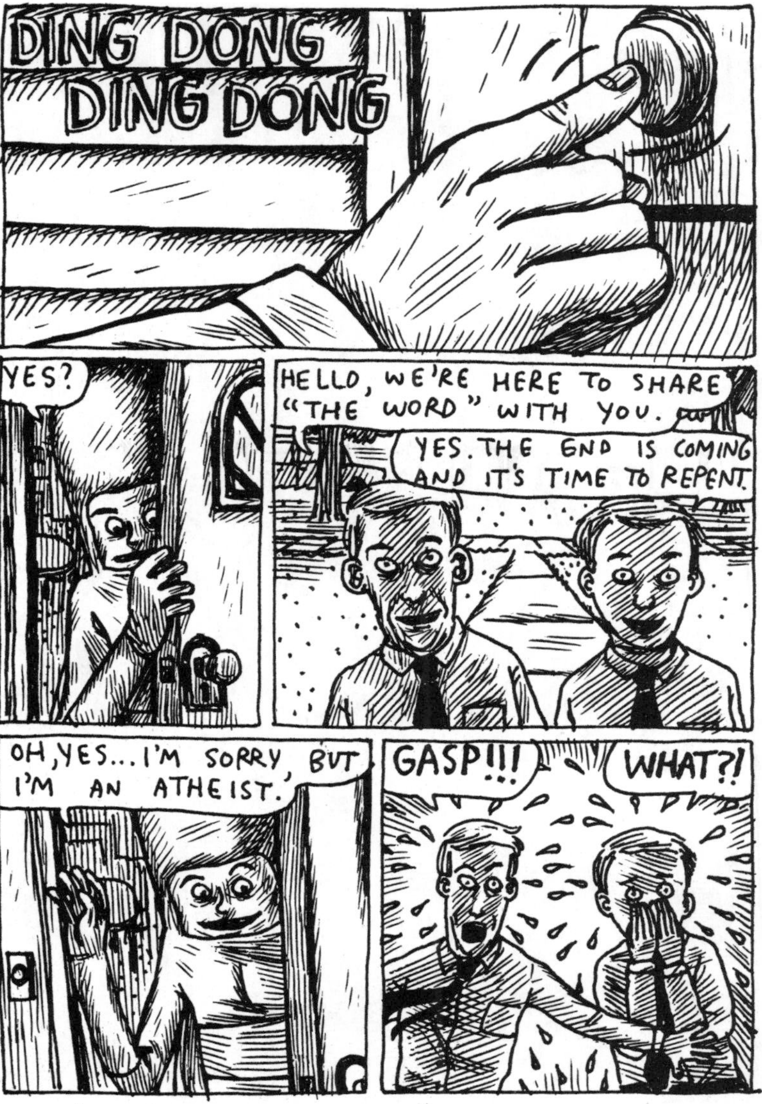
DING DONG
DING DONG
YES?
HELLO, WE'RE HERE TO SHARE "THE WORD" WITH YOU.
YES. THE END IS COMING AND IT'S TIME TO REPENT.
OH, YES... I'M SORRY, BUT I'M AN ATHEIST.
GASP!!!
WHAT?!

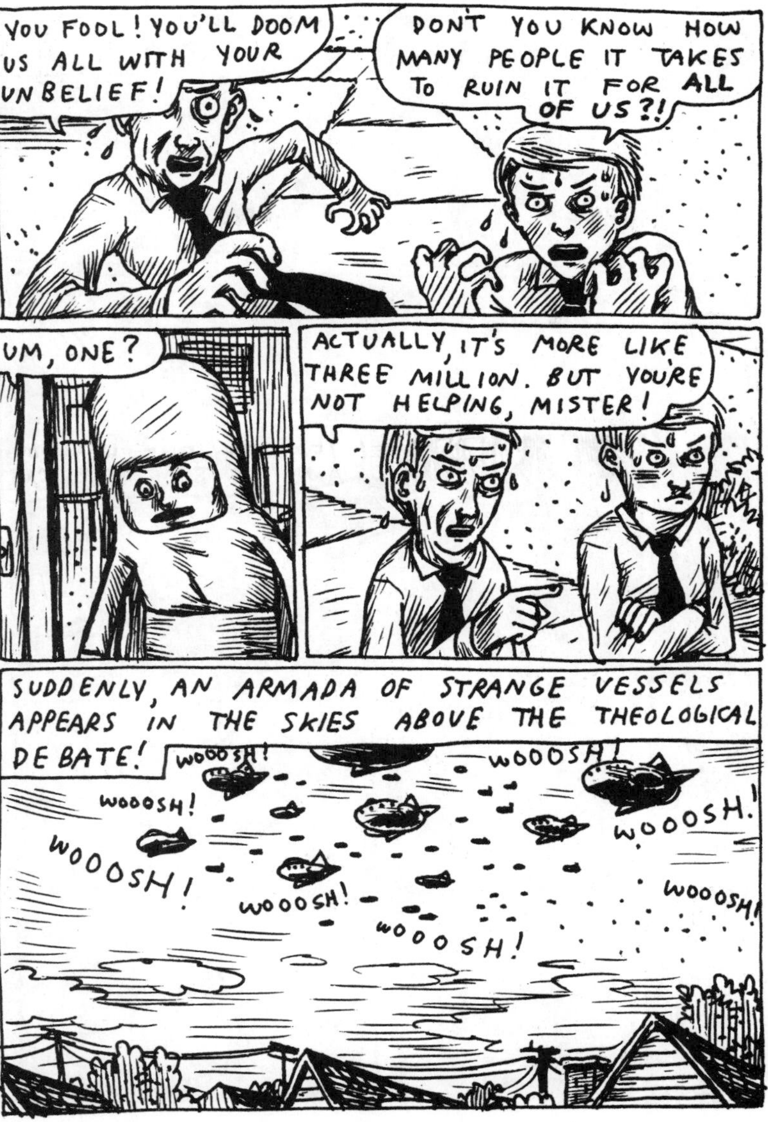
YOU FOOL! YOU'LL DOOM US ALL WITH YOUR UNBELIEF!
DON'T YOU KNOW HOW MANY PEOPLE IT TAKES TO RUIN IT FOR ALL OF US?!
UM, ONE?
ACTUALLY, IT'S MORE LIKE THREE MILLION. BUT YOU'RE NOT HELPING, MISTER!
SUDDENLY, AN ARMADA OF STRANGE VESSELS APPEARS IN THE SKIES ABOVE THE THEOLOGICAL DEBATE!
WOOOSH!
WOOOSH!
WOOOSH!
WOOOSH.
WOOOSH!
WOOOSH!
WOOOSH!
WOOOSH!
WOOOSH!

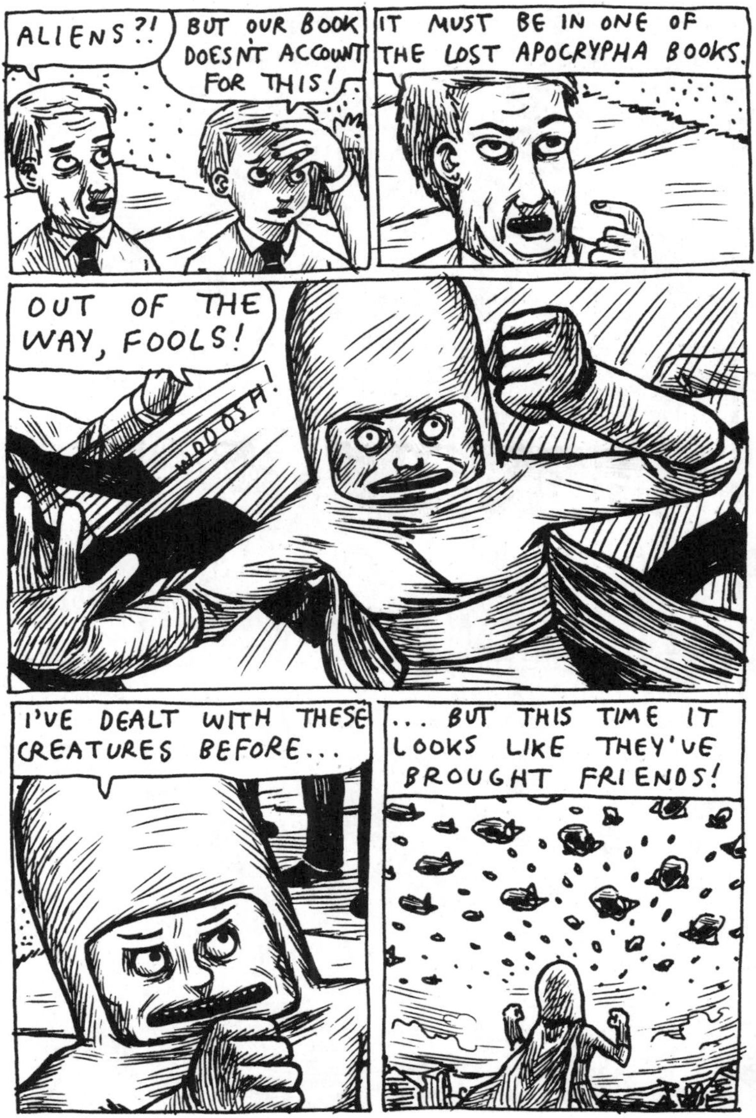
ALIENS?!
BUT OUR BOOK DOESN'T ACCOUNT FOR THIS!
IT MUST BE IN ONE OF THE LOST APOCRYPHA BOOKS.
OUT OF THE WAY, FOOLS!
WOOOSH!
I'VE DEALT WITH THESE CREATURES BEFORE...
... BUT THIS TIME IT LOOKS LIKE THEY'VE BROUGHT FRIENDS!

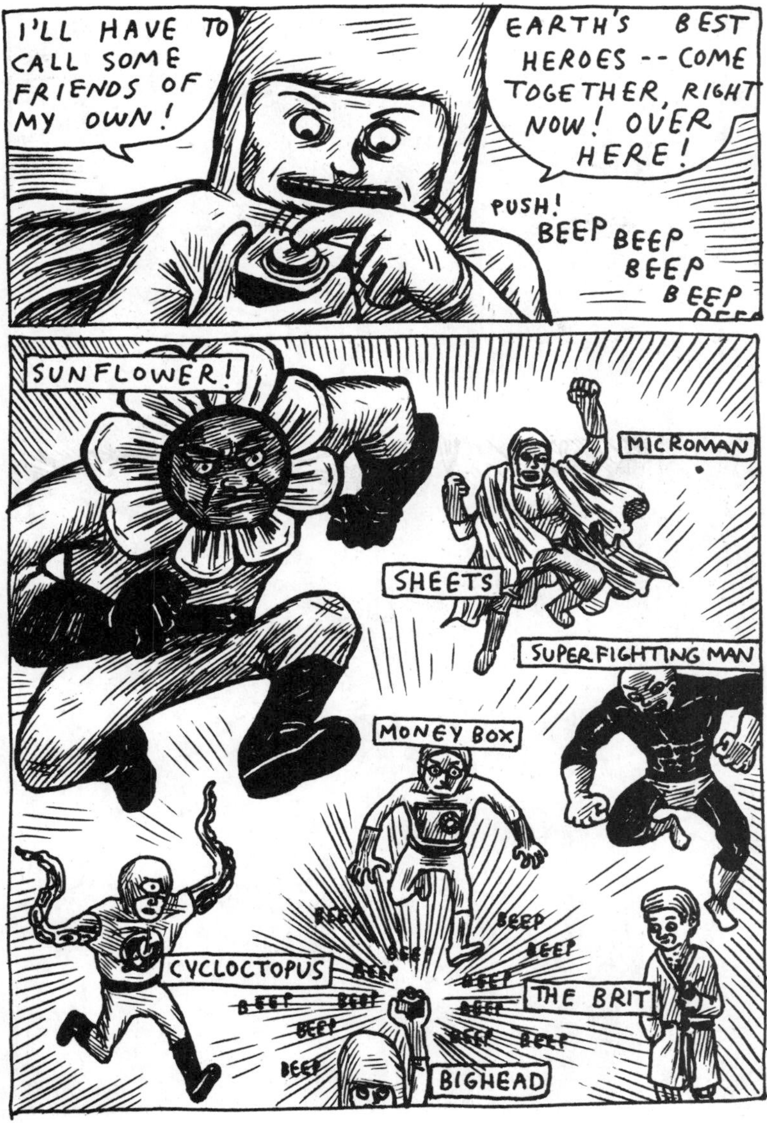
I'LL HAVE TO CALL SOME FRIENDS OF MY OWN!
EARTH'S BEST HEROES -- COME TOGETHER, RIGHT NOW! OVER HERE!
PUSH!
BEEP BEEP BEEP BEEP
SUNFLOWER!
MICROMAN
SHEETS
SUPERFIGHTING MAN
MONEY BOX
CYCLOCTOPUS
THE BRIT
BIGHEAD
BEEP
BEEP
BEEP

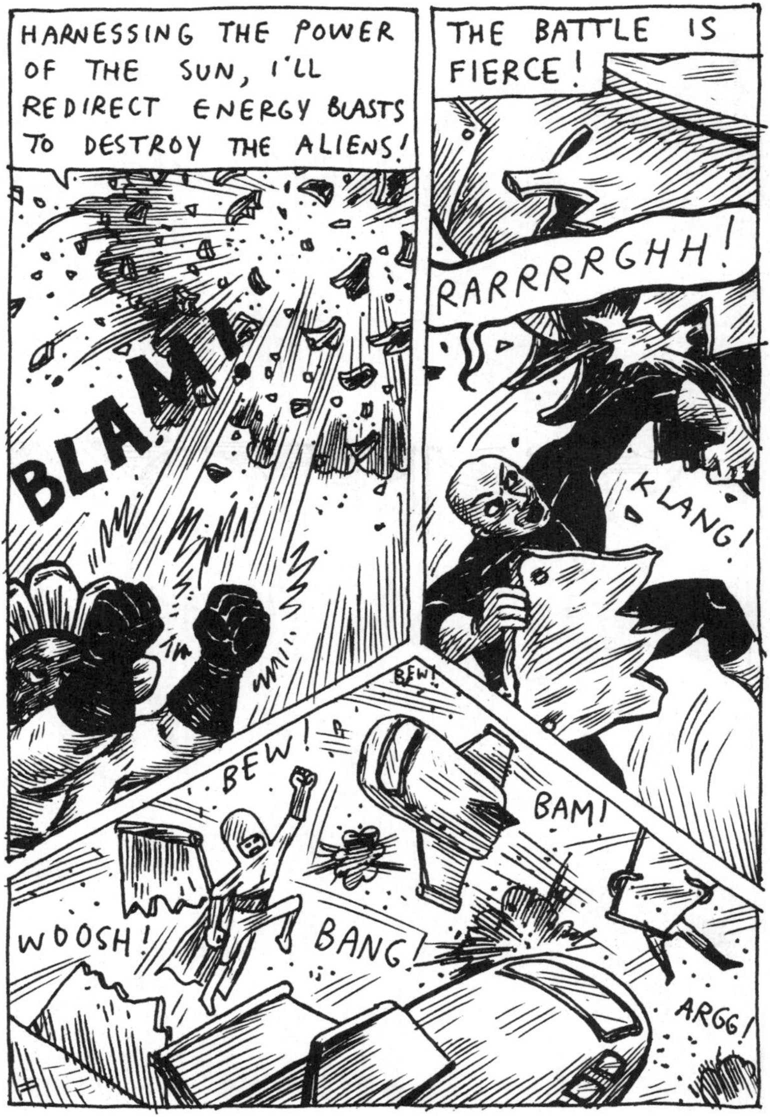
HARNESSING THE POWER OF THE SUN, I'LL REDIRECT ENERGY BLASTS TO DESTROY THE ALIENS!
BLAM!
THE BATTLE IS FIERCE!
RARRRRRGHH!
KLANG!
BEW!
BEW!
BAM!
WOOSH!
BANG!
ARGG!

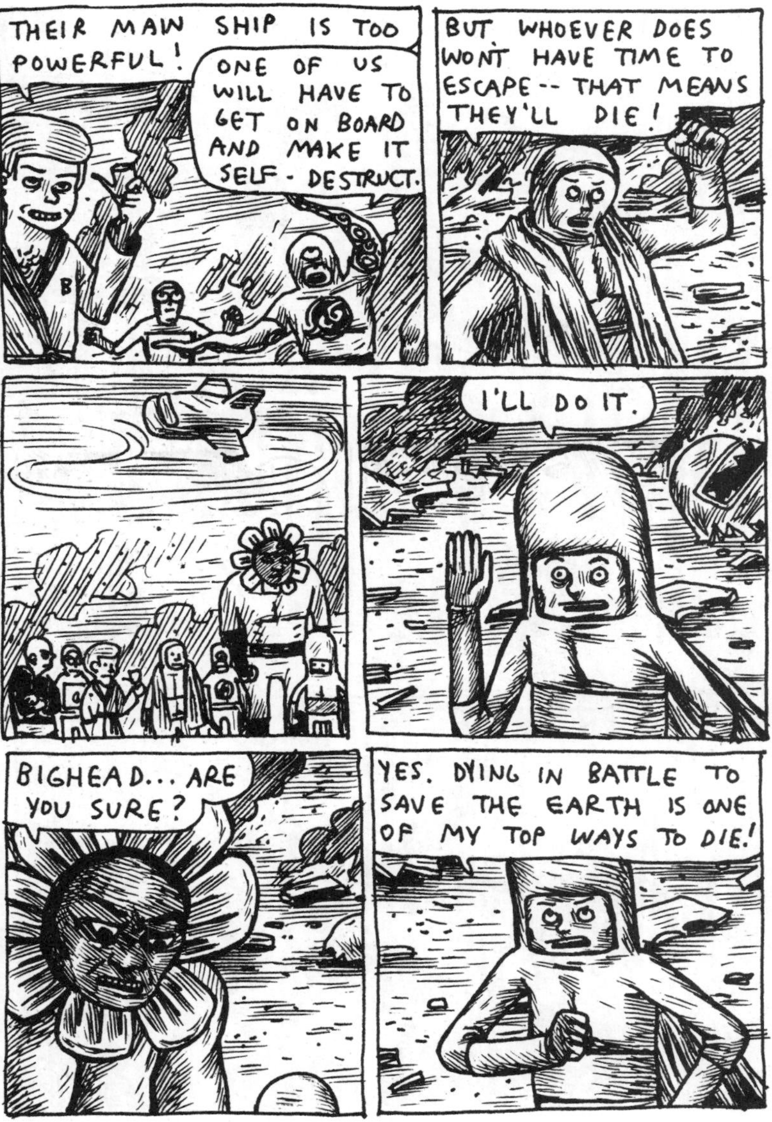
THEIR MAIN SHIP IS TOO POWERFUL!
ONE OF US WILL HAVE TO GET ON BOARD AND MAKE IT SELF-DESTRUCT.
BUT WHOEVER DOES WON'T HAVE TIME TO ESCAPE-- THAT MEANS THEY'LL DIE!
I'LL DO IT.
BIGHEAD... ARE YOU SURE?
YES. DYING IN BATTLE TO SAVE THE EARTH IS ONE OF MY TOP WAYS TO DIE!

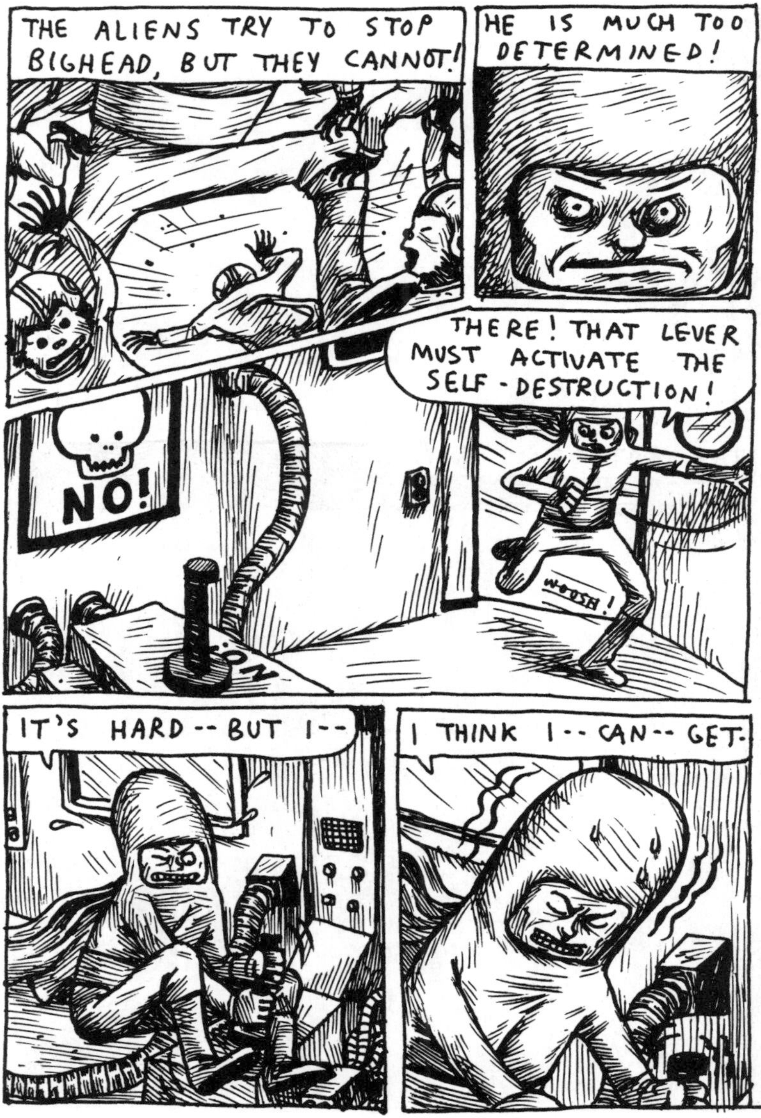
THE ALIENS TRY TO STOP BIGHEAD, BUT THEY CANNOT!
HE IS MUCH TOO DETERMINED!
THERE! THAT LEVER MUST ACTIVATE THE SELF-DESTRUCTION!
NO!
WOOSH!
ON
IT'S HARD-- BUT I--
I THINK I-- CAN-- GET-

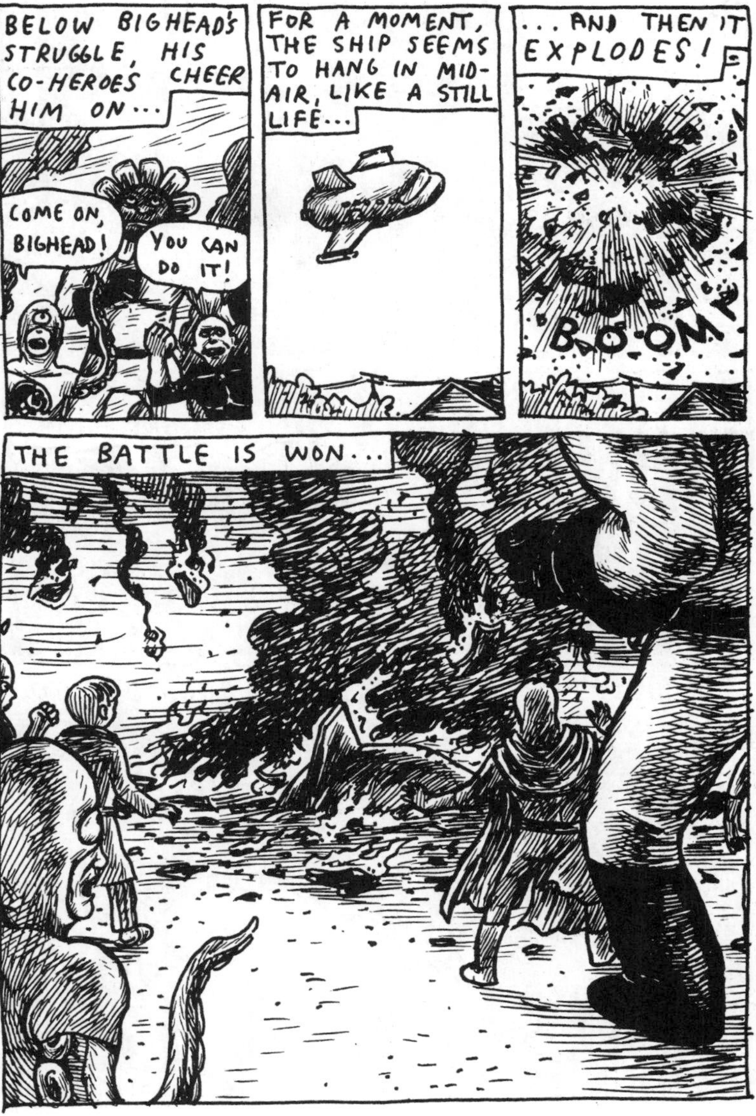
BELOW BIGHEAD'S STRUGGLE, HIS CO-HEROES CHEER HIM ON...
COME ON, BIGHEAD!
YOU CAN DO IT!
FOR A MOMENT, THE SHIP SEEMS TO HANG IN MID-AIR, LIKE A STILL LIFE...
...AND THEN IT EXPLODES!
BOOM
THE BATTLE IS WON...

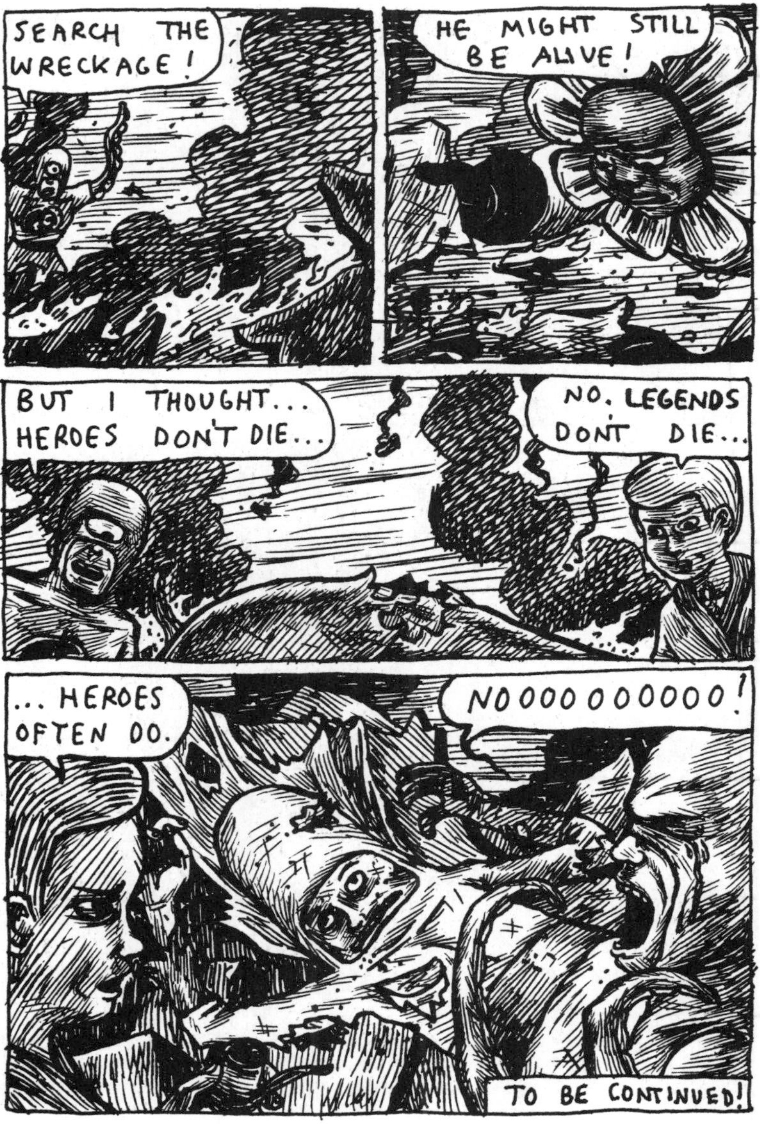
SEARCH THE WRECKAGE!
HE MIGHT STILL BE ALIVE!
BUT I THOUGHT... HEROES DON'T DIE...
NO. LEGENDS DONT DIE...
... HEROES OFTEN DO.
NOOOOOOOOOOO!
TO BE CONTINUED!

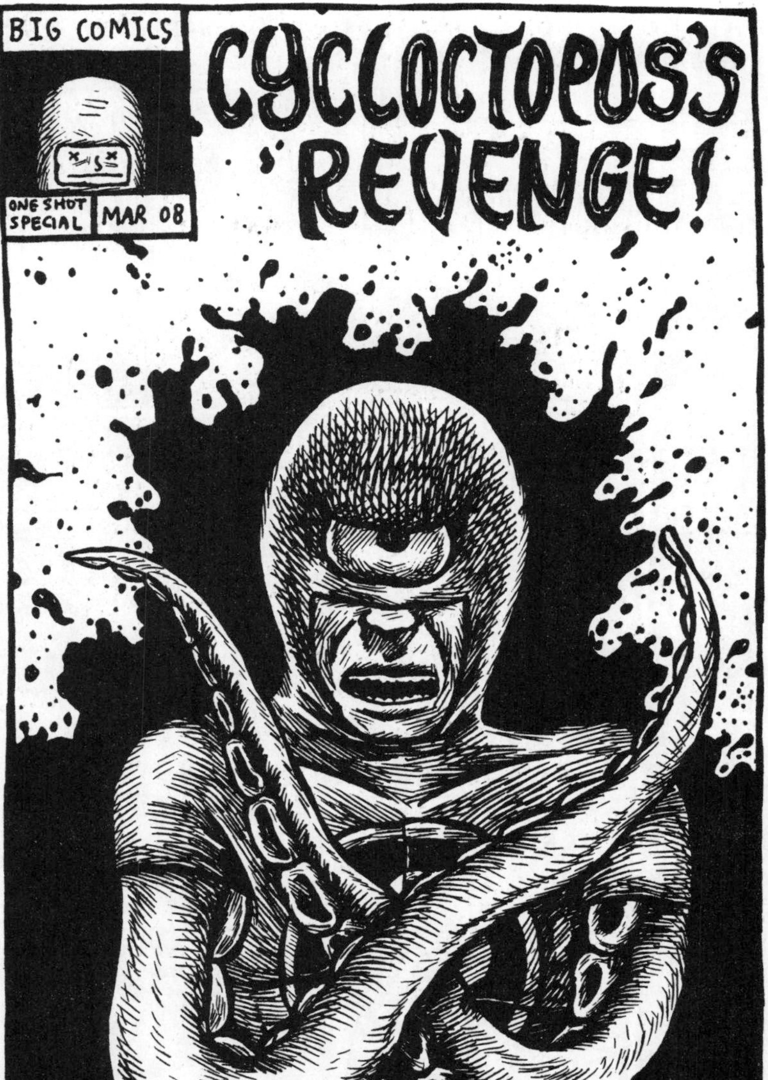
BIG COMICS
ONE SHOT SPECIAL
MAR 08
CYCLOCTOPUS'S REVENGE!

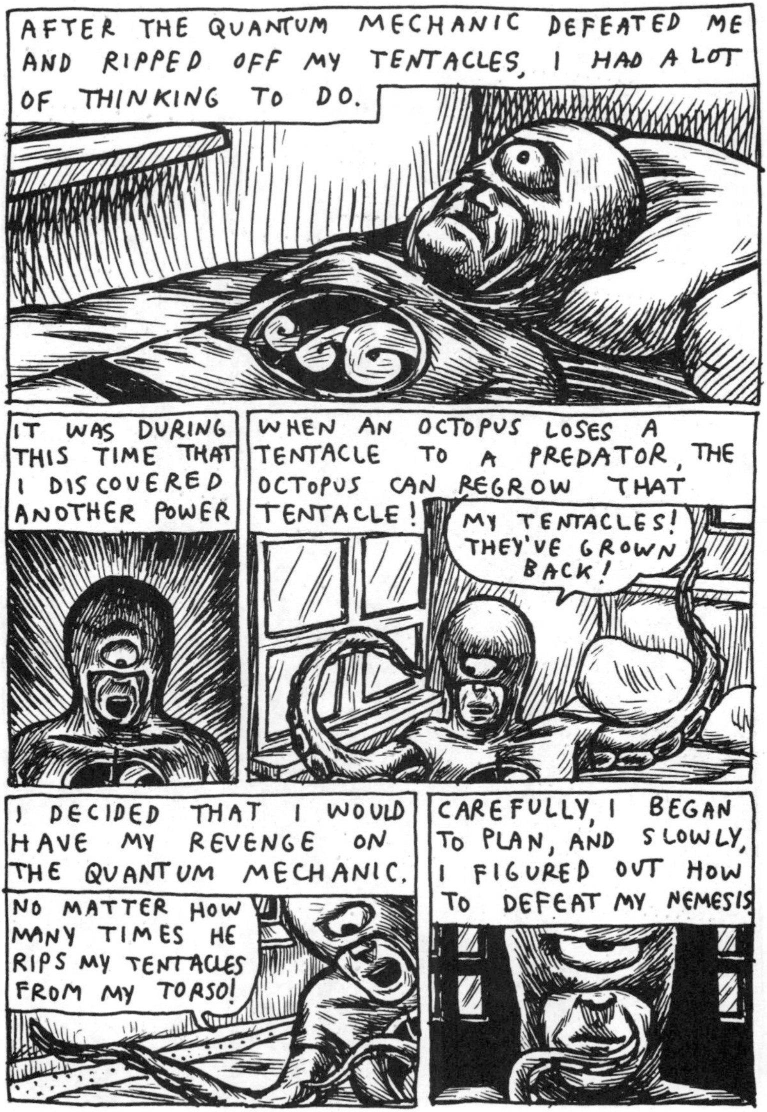
AFTER THE QUANTUM MECHANIC DEFEATED ME AND RIPPED OFF MY TENTACLES, I HAD A LOT OF THINKING TO DO.
IT WAS DURING THIS TIME THAT I DISCOVERED ANOTHER POWER
WHEN AN OCTOPUS LOSES A TENTACLE TO A PREDATOR, THE OCTOPUS CAN REGROW THAT TENTACLE!
MY TENTACLES! THEY'VE GROWN BACK!
I DECIDED THAT I WOULD HAVE MY REVENGE ON THE QUANTUM MECHANIC.
NO MATTER HOW MANY TIMES HE RIPS MY TENTACLES FROM MY TORSO!
CAREFULLY, I BEGAN TO PLAN, AND SLOWLY, I FIGURED OUT HOW TO DEFEAT MY NEMESIS

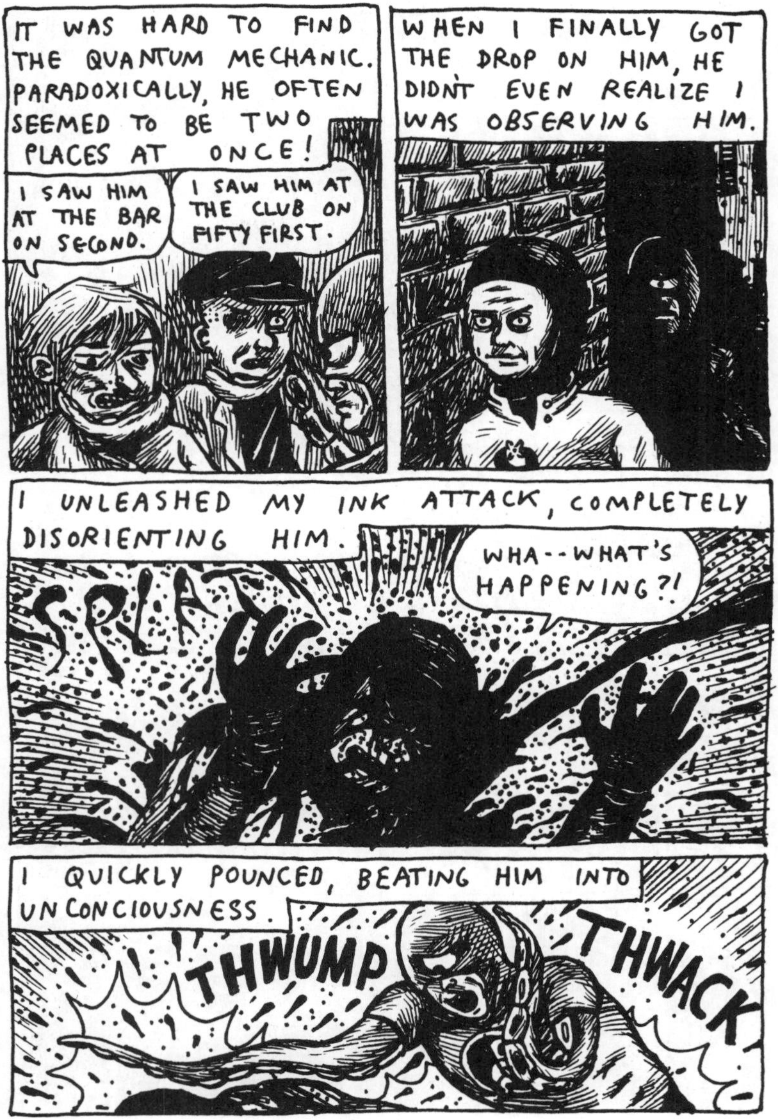
IT WAS HARD TO FIND THE QUANTUM MECHANIC. PARADOXICALLY, HE OFTEN SEEMED TO BE TWO PLACES AT ONCE!
I SAW HIM AT THE BAR ON SECOND.
I SAW HIM AT THE CLUB ON FIFTY FIRST.
WHEN I FINALLY GOT THE DROP ON HIM, HE DIDN'T EVEN REALIZE I WAS OBSERVING HIM.
I UNLEASHED MY INK ATTACK, COMPLETELY DISORIENTING HIM.
SPLAT
WHA--WHAT'S HAPPENING?!
I QUICKLY POUNCED, BEATING HIM INTO UNCONCIOUSNESS.
THWUMP
THWACK

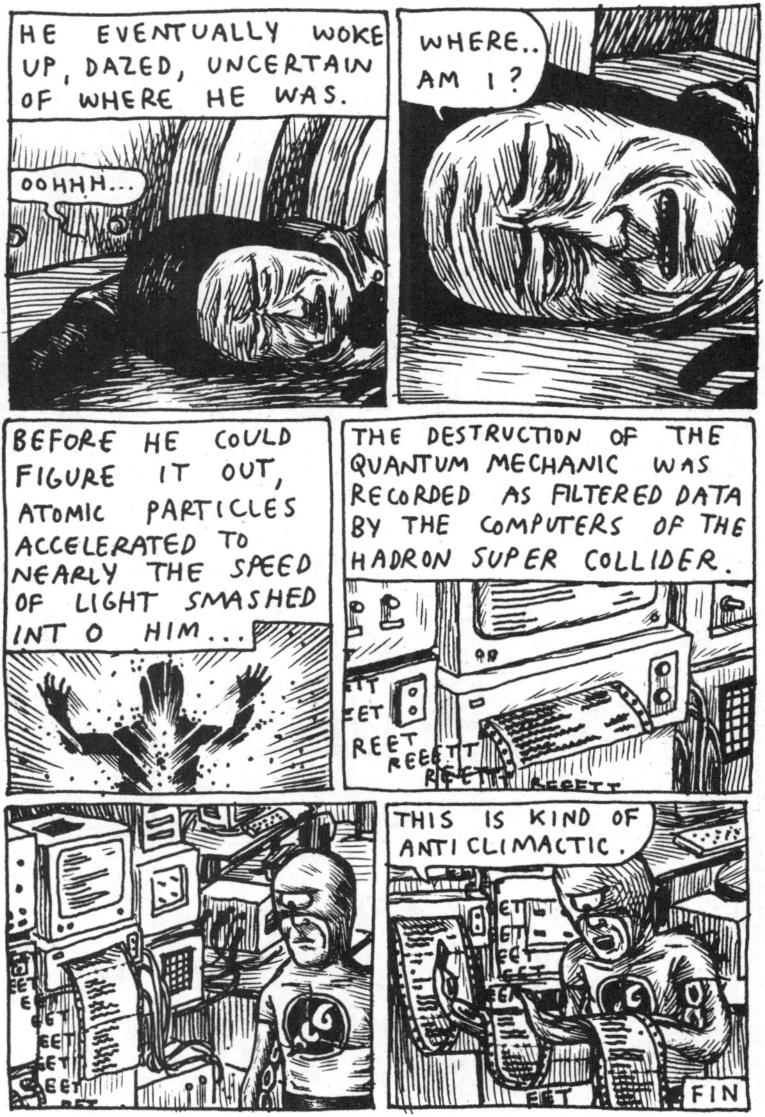
HE EVENTUALLY WOKE UP, DAZED, UNCERTAIN OF WHERE HE WAS.
OOHHH...
WHERE.. AM I?
BEFORE HE COULD FIGURE IT OUT, ATOMIC PARTICLES ACCELERATED TO NEARLY THE SPEED OF LIGHT SMASHED INT O HIM...
THE DESTRUCTION OF THE QUANTUM MECHANIC WAS RECORDED AS FILTERED DATA BY THE COMPUTERS OF THE HADRON SUPER COLLIDER.
REET
THIS IS KIND OF ANTI CLIMACTIC.
FIN

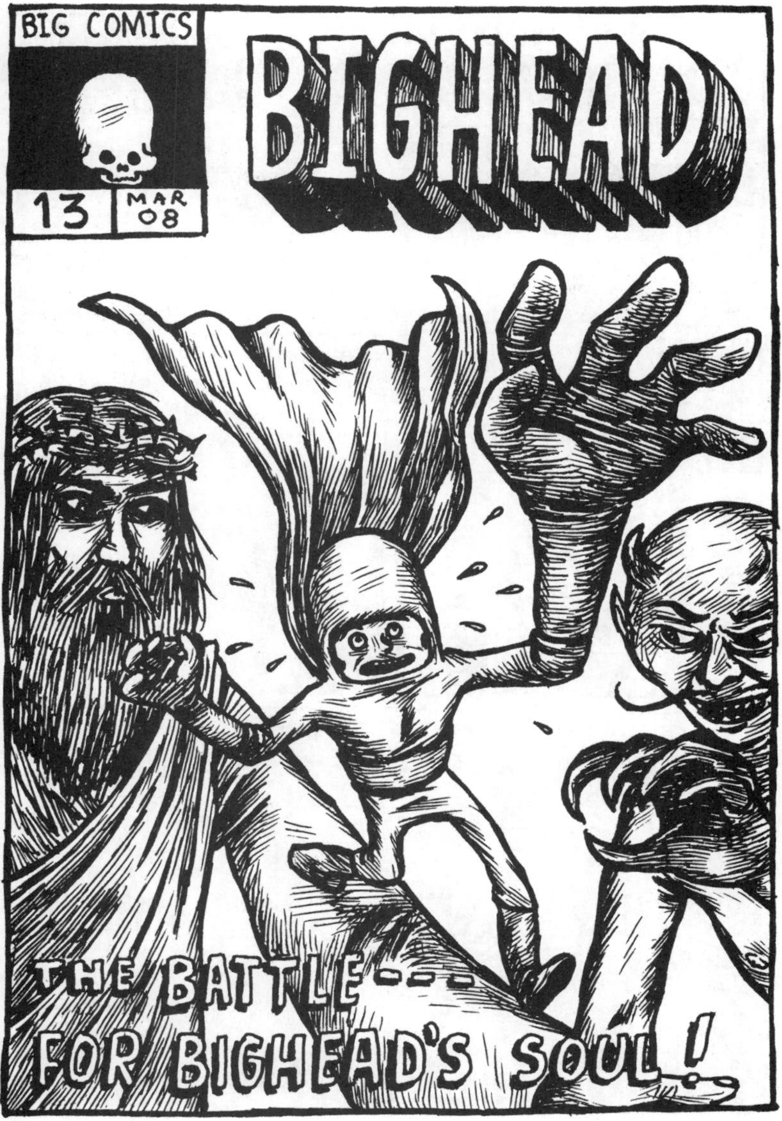
BIG COMICS
13
MAR 08
BIGHEAD
THE BATTLE---
FOR BIGHEAD'S SOUL!

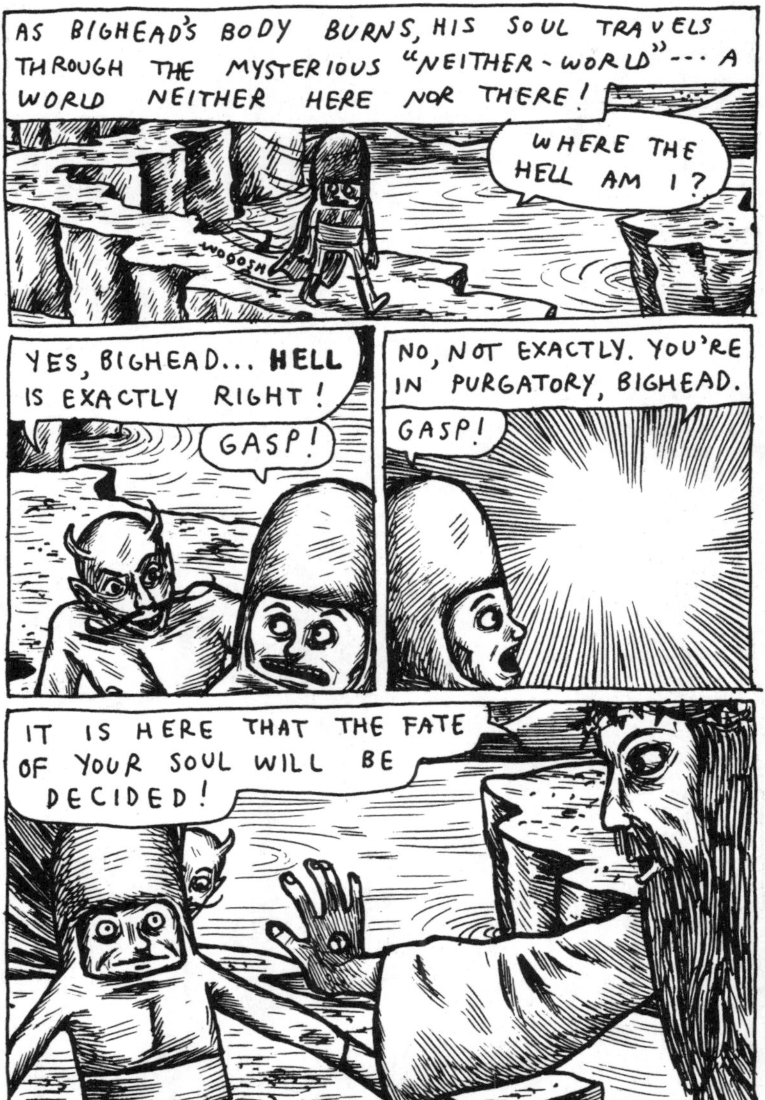
AS BIGHEAD'S BODY BURNS, HIS SOUL TRAVELS THROUGH THE MYSTERIOUS "NEITHER-WORLD"--- A WORLD NEITHER HERE NOR THERE!
WHERE THE HELL AM I?
WOOOSH
YES, BIGHEAD... **HELL** IS EXACTLY RIGHT!
GASP!
NO, NOT EXACTLY. YOU'RE IN PURGATORY, BIGHEAD.
GASP!
IT IS HERE THAT THE FATE OF YOUR SOUL WILL BE DECIDED!

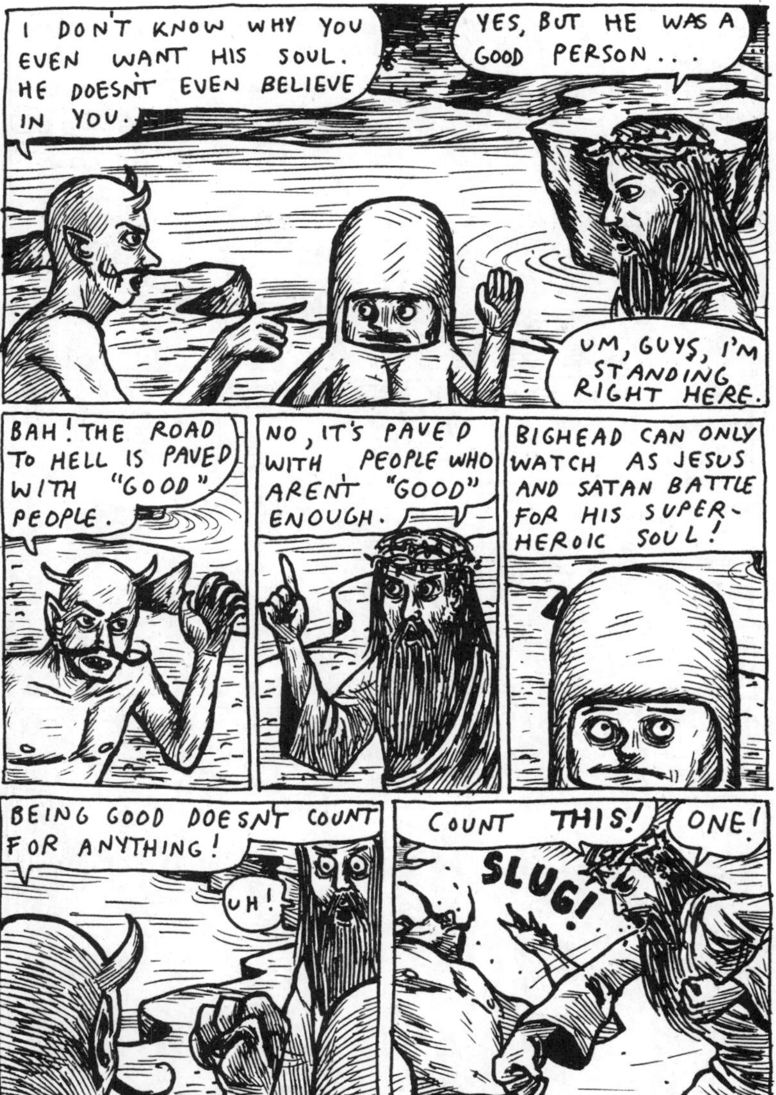
I DON'T KNOW WHY YOU EVEN WANT HIS SOUL. HE DOESN'T EVEN BELIEVE IN YOU.
YES, BUT HE WAS A GOOD PERSON...
UM, GUYS, I'M STANDING RIGHT HERE.
BAH! THE ROAD TO HELL IS PAVED WITH "GOOD" PEOPLE.
NO, IT'S PAVED WITH PEOPLE WHO AREN'T "GOOD" ENOUGH.
BIGHEAD CAN ONLY WATCH AS JESUS AND SATAN BATTLE FOR HIS SUPER-HEROIC SOUL!
BEING GOOD DOESN'T COUNT FOR ANYTHING!
UH!
COUNT THIS!
ONE!
SLUG!

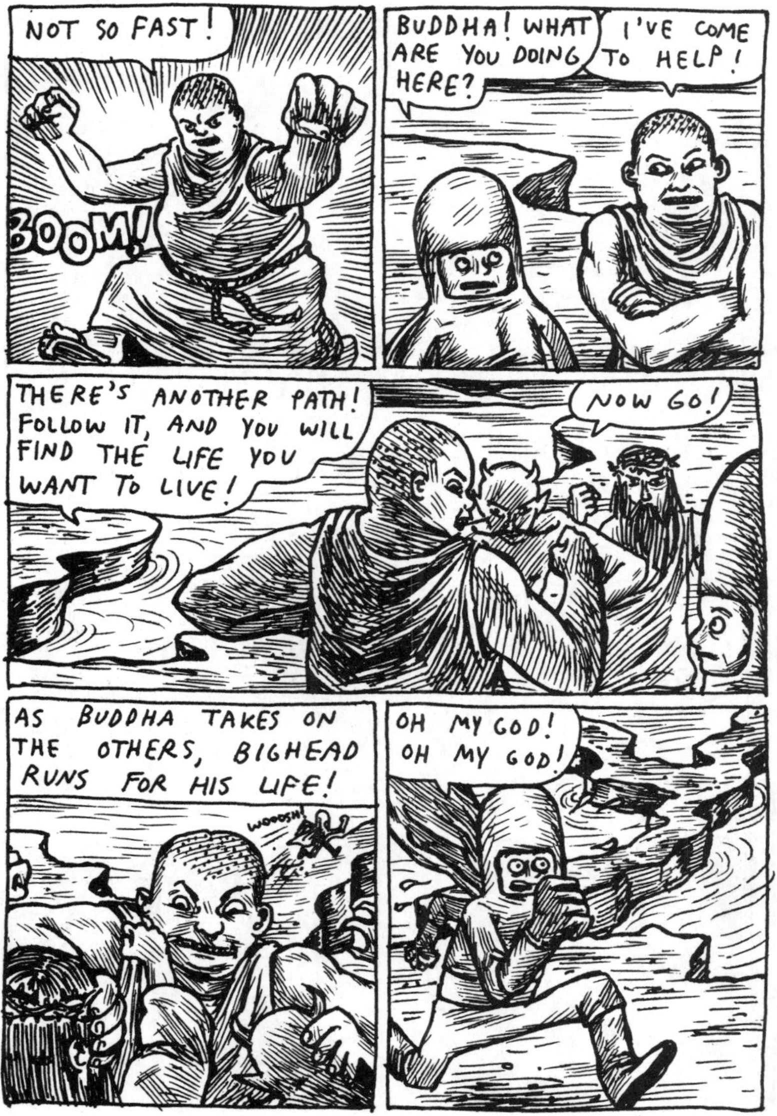
NOT SO FAST!
BOOM!
BUDDHA! WHAT ARE YOU DOING HERE?
I'VE COME TO HELP!
THERE'S ANOTHER PATH! FOLLOW IT, AND YOU WILL FIND THE LIFE YOU WANT TO LIVE!
NOW GO!
AS BUDDHA TAKES ON THE OTHERS, BIGHEAD RUNS FOR HIS LIFE!
WOOOSH!
OH MY GOD! OH MY GOD!

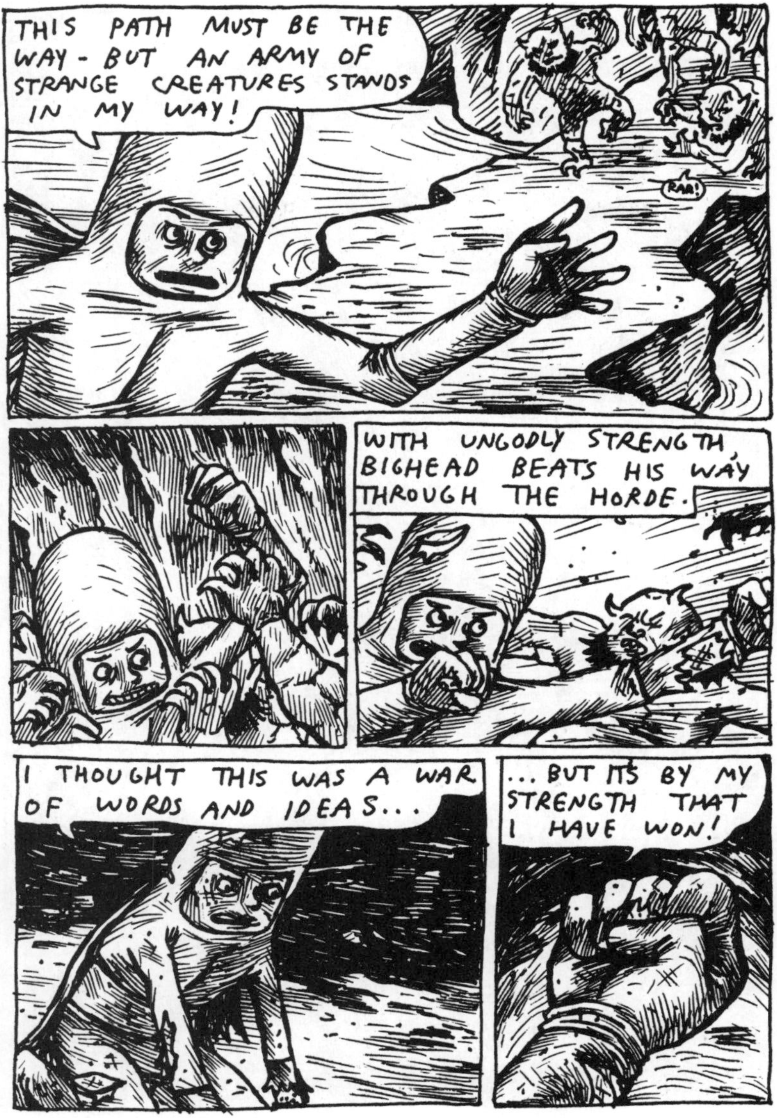
THIS PATH MUST BE THE WAY - BUT AN ARMY OF STRANGE CREATURES STANDS IN MY WAY!
RAA!
WITH UNGODLY STRENGTH BIGHEAD BEATS HIS WAY THROUGH THE HORDE.
I THOUGHT THIS WAS A WAR OF WORDS AND IDEAS...
...BUT IT'S BY MY STRENGTH THAT I HAVE WON!

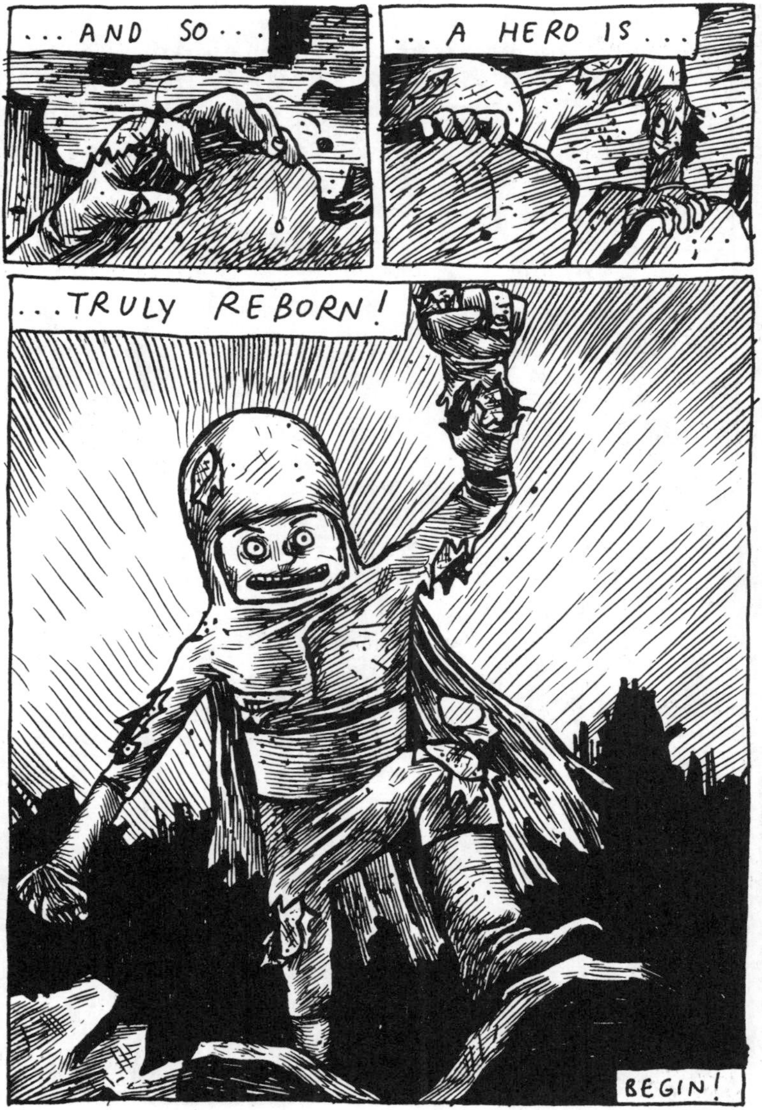

...AND SO...
...A HERO IS...
...TRULY REBORN!
BEGIN!

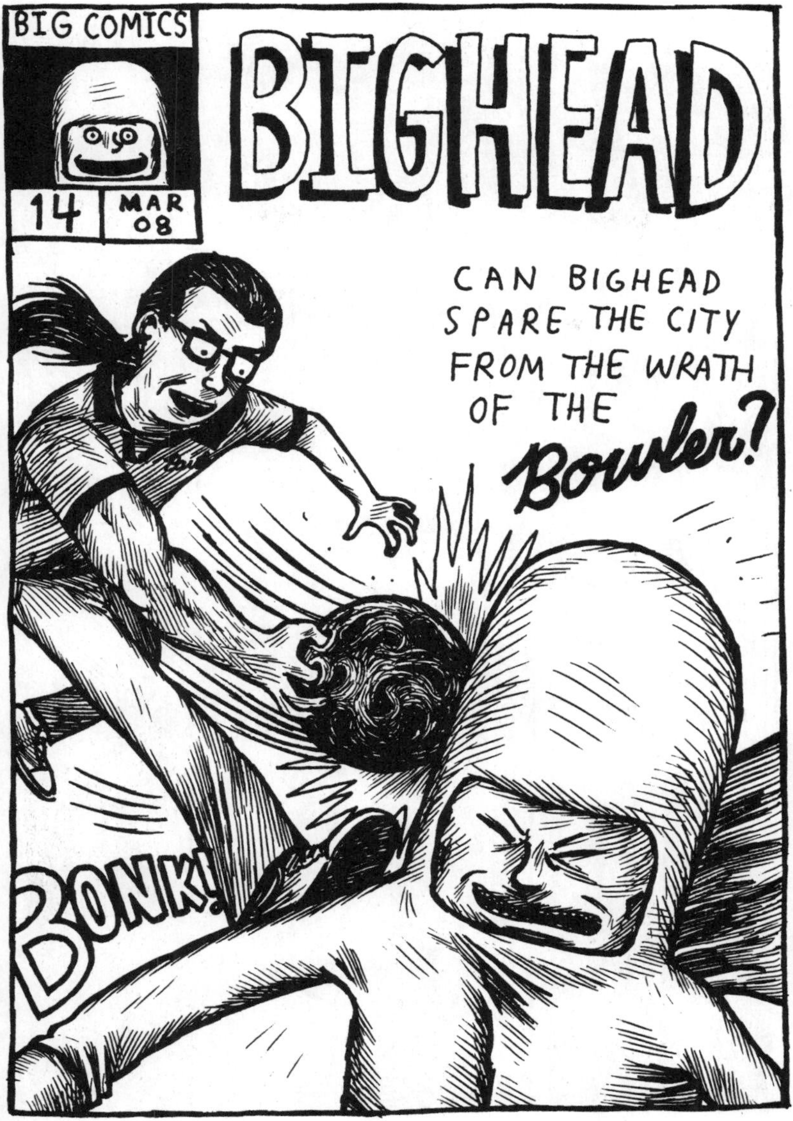
BIG COMICS
BIGHEAD
14
MAR 08
CAN BIGHEAD SPARE THE CITY FROM THE WRATH OF THE Bowler?
BONK!

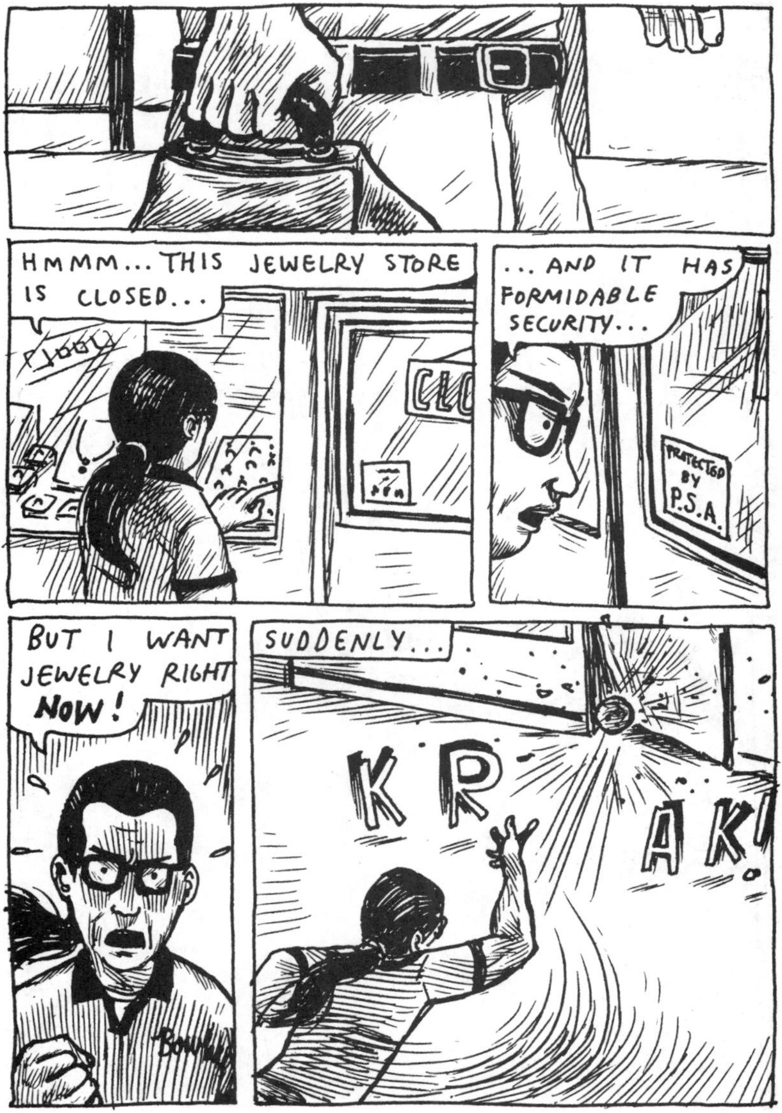

HMMM... THIS JEWELRY STORE IS CLOSED...
CLO
... AND IT HAS FORMIDABLE SECURITY...
PROTECTED BY P.S.A.
BUT I WANT JEWELRY RIGHT NOW!
SUDDENLY...
KR
AK

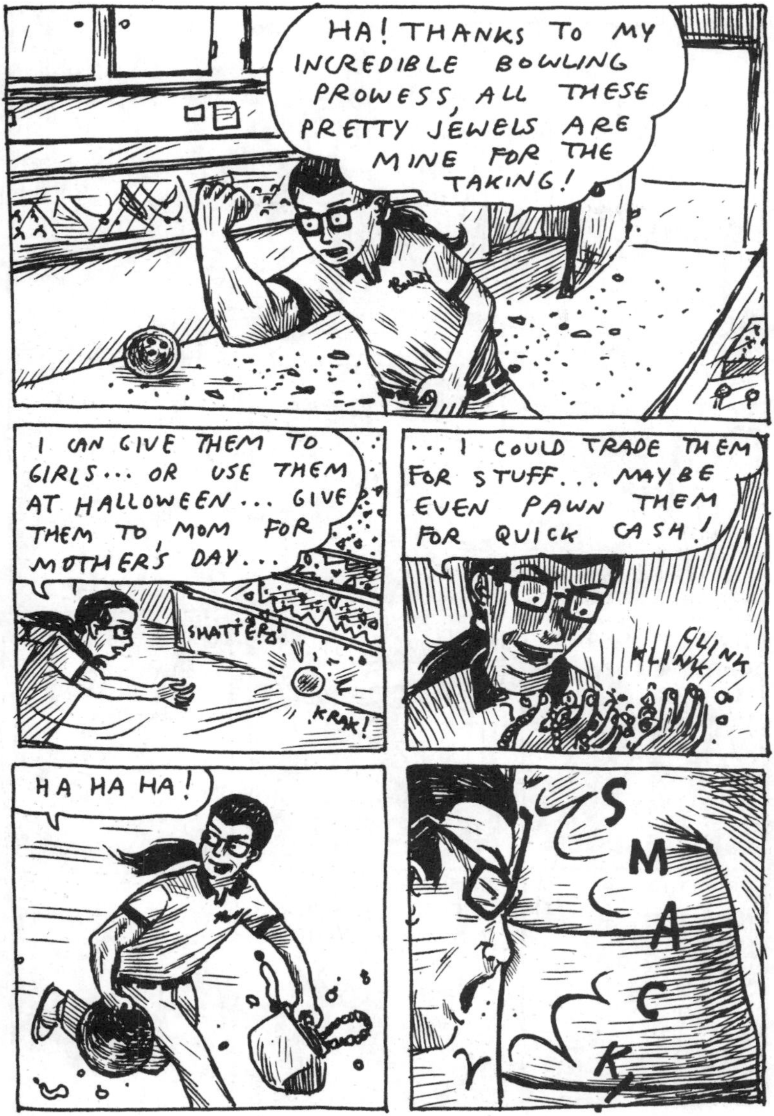
HA! THANKS TO MY INCREDIBLE BOWLING PROWESS, ALL THESE PRETTY JEWELS ARE MINE FOR THE TAKING!
I CAN GIVE THEM TO GIRLS... OR USE THEM AT HALLOWEEN... GIVE THEM TO MOM FOR MOTHER'S DAY...
SHATTER!
KRAK!
...I COULD TRADE THEM FOR STUFF... MAYBE EVEN PAWN THEM FOR QUICK CASH!
CLINK
KLINK
HA HA HA!
SMACK!

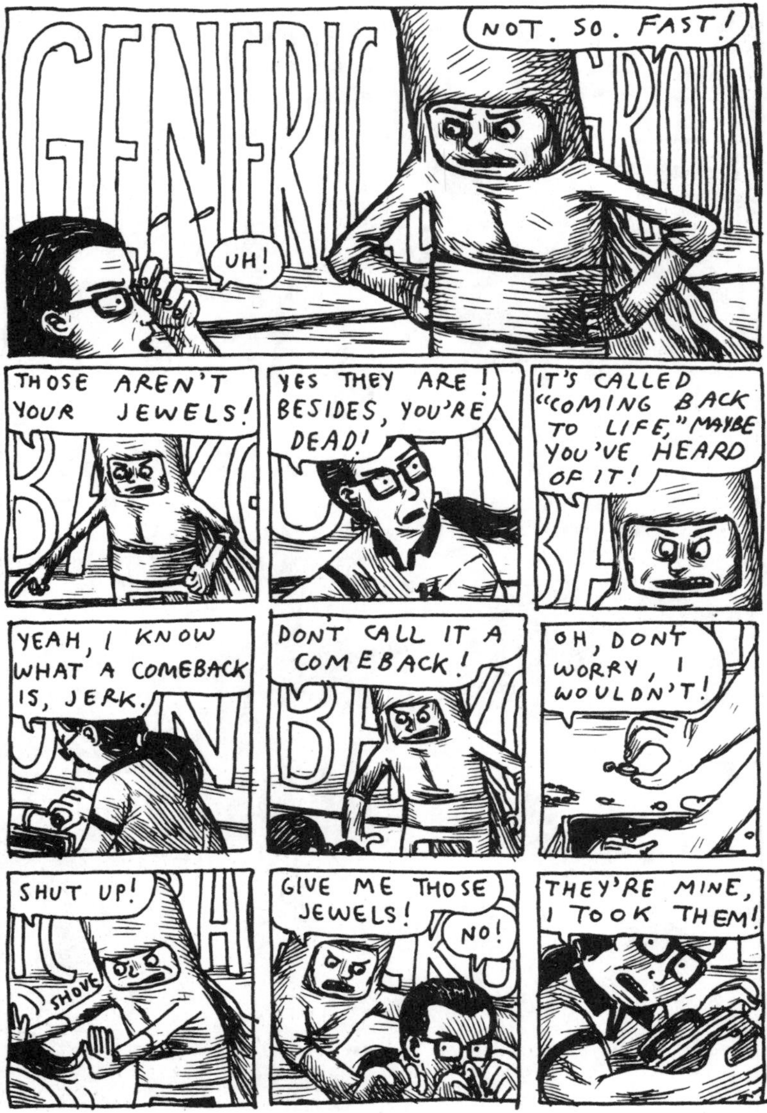
GENERIC
NOT. SO. FAST!
UH!
THOSE AREN'T YOUR JEWELS!
YES THEY ARE! BESIDES, YOU'RE DEAD!
IT'S CALLED "COMING BACK TO LIFE," MAYBE YOU'VE HEARD OF IT!
YEAH, I KNOW WHAT A COMEBACK IS, JERK.
DON'T CALL IT A COMEBACK!
OH, DON'T WORRY, I WOULDN'T!
SHUT UP!
SHOVE
GIVE ME THOSE JEWELS!
NO!
THEY'RE MINE, I TOOK THEM!

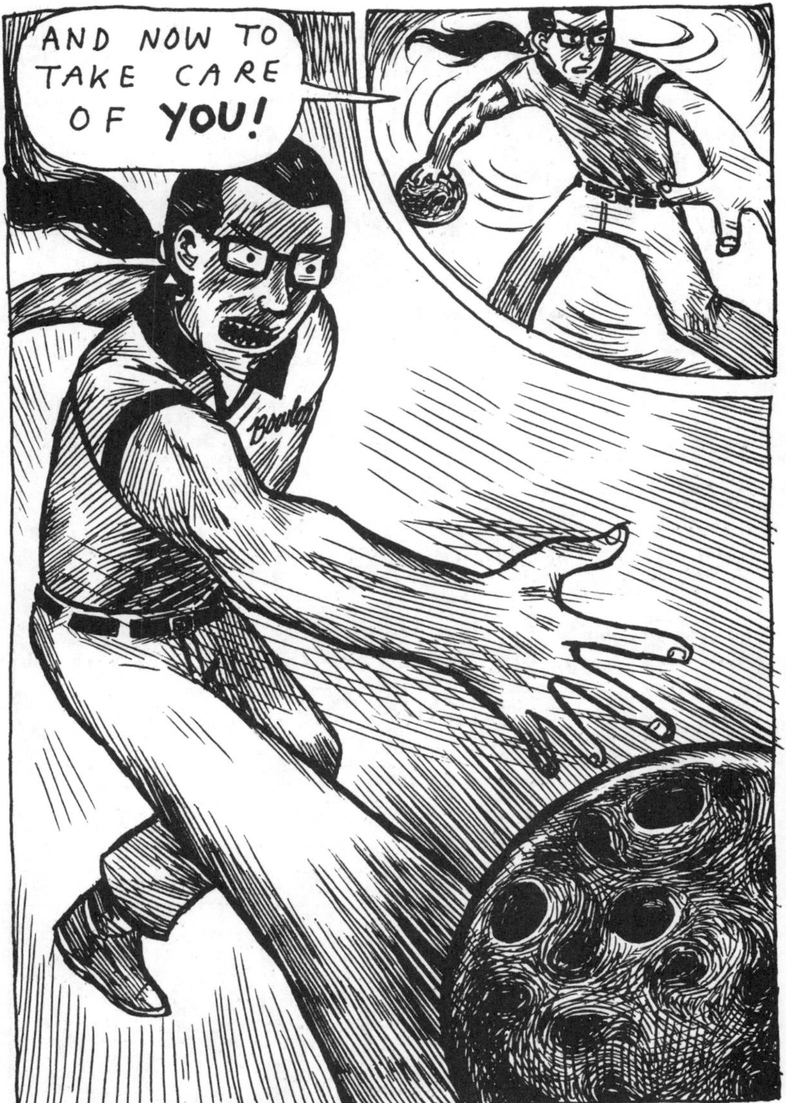
AND NOW TO TAKE CARE OF YOU!
Bowler

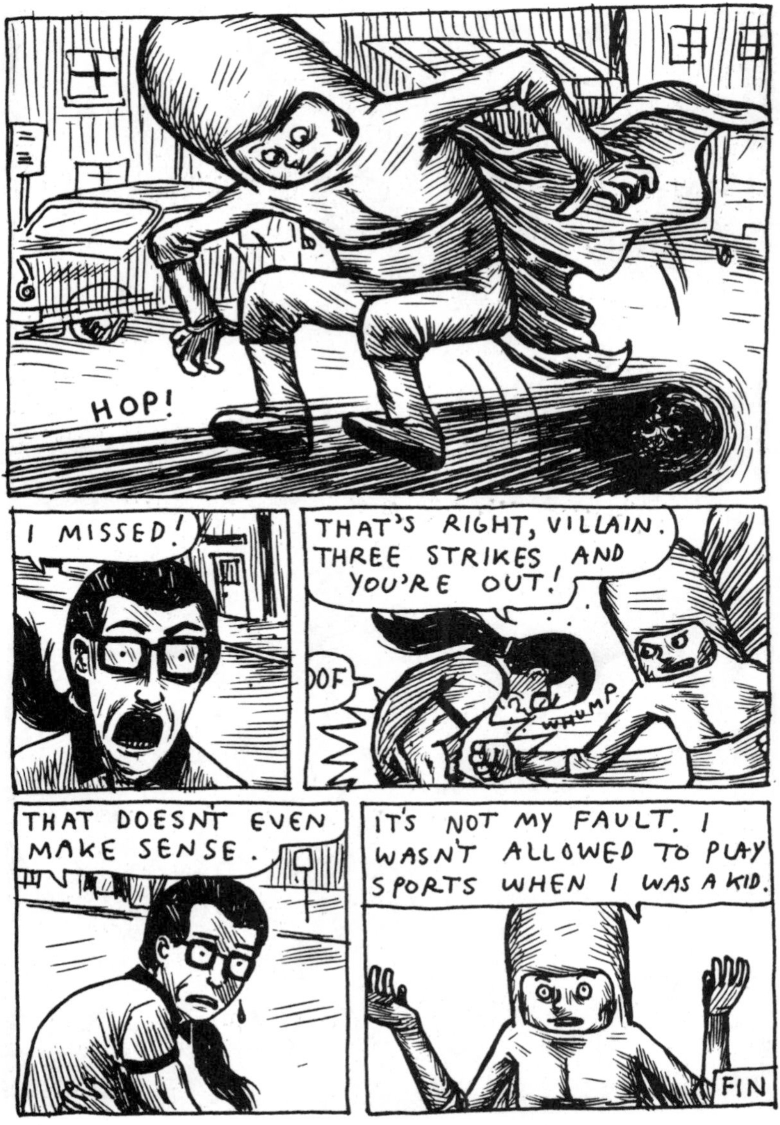
HOP!
I MISSED!
THAT'S RIGHT, VILLAIN. THREE STRIKES AND YOU'RE OUT!
OF
WHUMP
THAT DOESN'T EVEN MAKE SENSE.
IT'S NOT MY FAULT. I WASN'T ALLOWED TO PLAY SPORTS WHEN I WAS A KID.
FIN

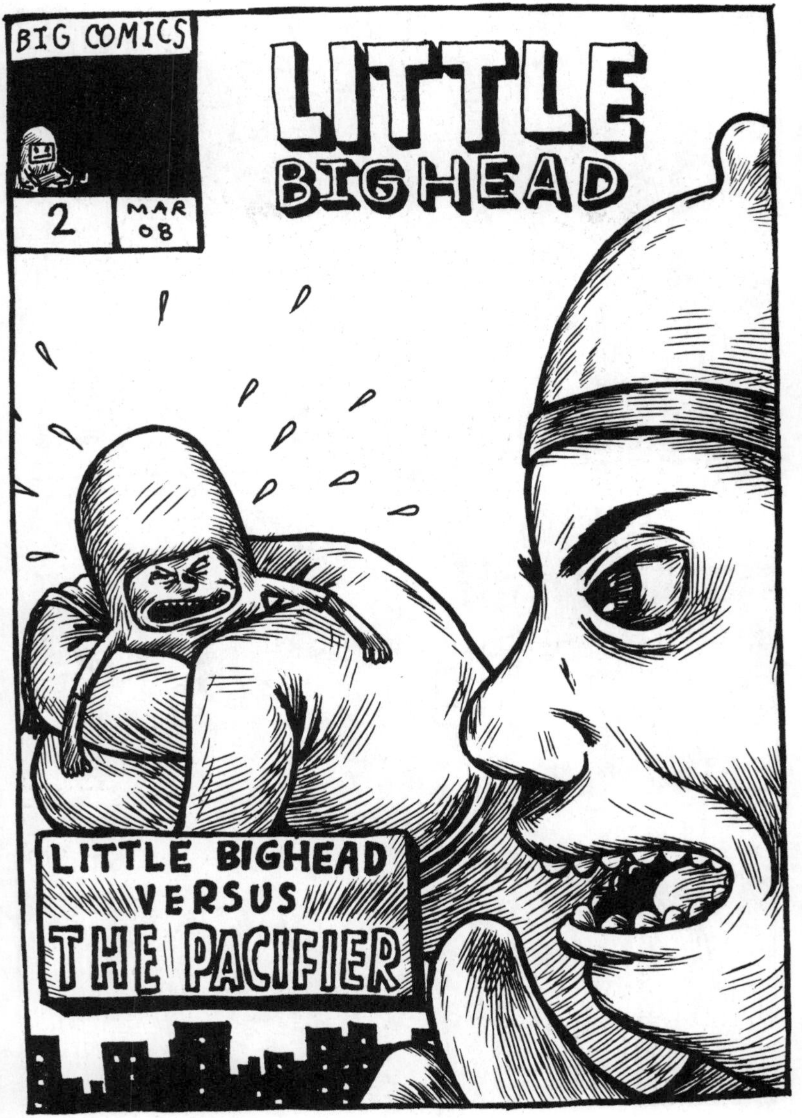
BIG COMICS
2
MAR 08
LITTLE BIGHEAD
LITTLE BIGHEAD VERSUS THE PACIFIER

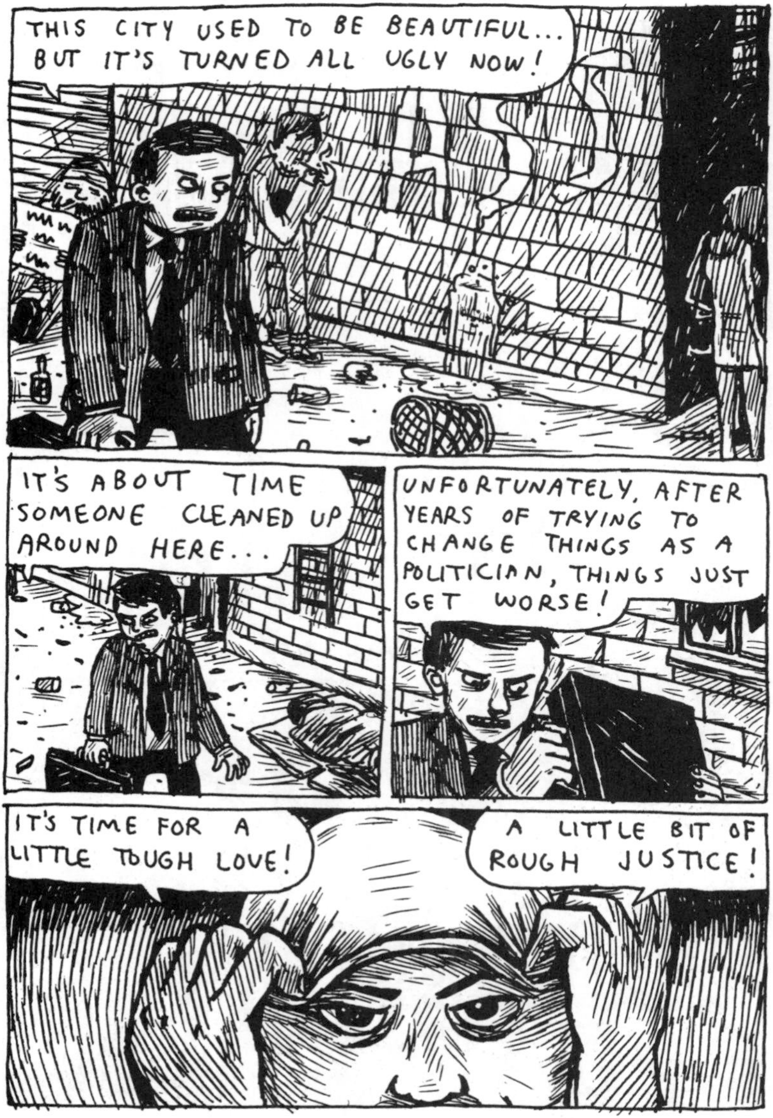
THIS CITY USED TO BE BEAUTIFUL... BUT IT'S TURNED ALL UGLY NOW!
IT'S ABOUT TIME SOMEONE CLEANED UP AROUND HERE...
UNFORTUNATELY, AFTER YEARS OF TRYING TO CHANGE THINGS AS A POLITICIAN, THINGS JUST GET WORSE!
IT'S TIME FOR A LITTLE TOUGH LOVE!
A LITTLE BIT OF ROUGH JUSTICE!

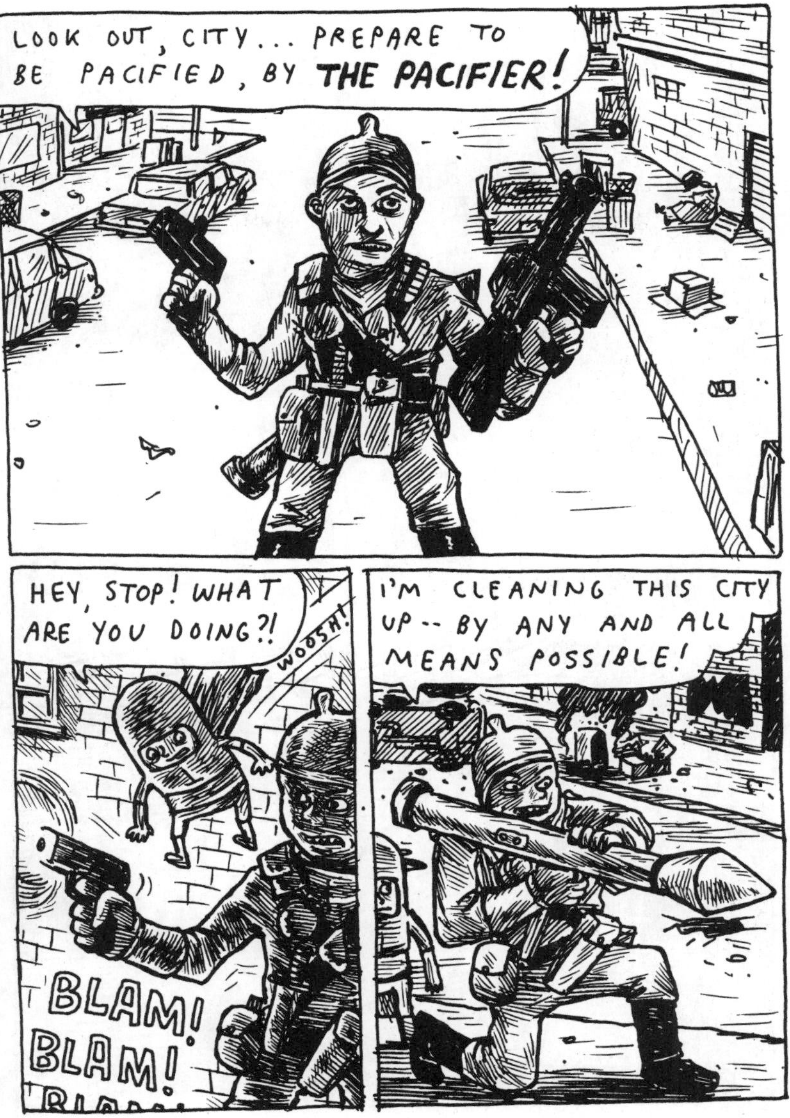
LOOK OUT, CITY... PREPARE TO BE PACIFIED, BY THE PACIFIER!
HEY, STOP! WHAT ARE YOU DOING?!
WOOSH!
BLAM! BLAM!
I'M CLEANING THIS CITY UP-- BY ANY AND ALL MEANS POSSIBLE!

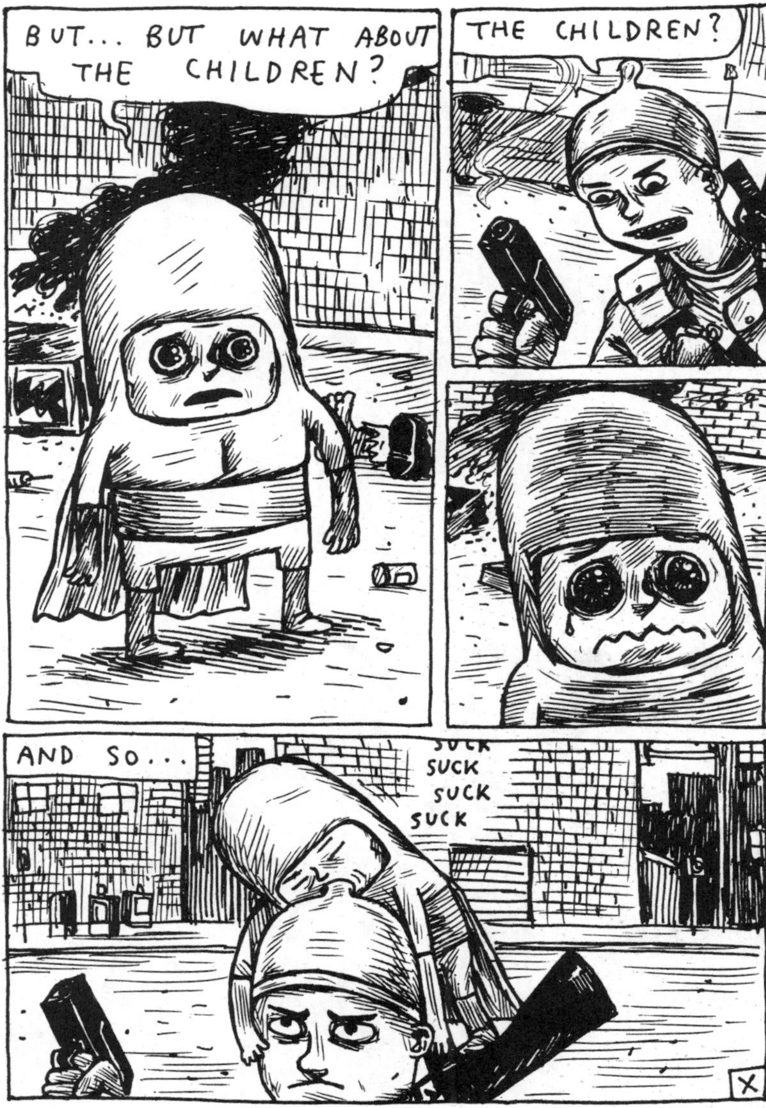
BUT... BUT WHAT ABOUT THE CHILDREN?
THE CHILDREN?
AND SO...
SUCK
SUCK
SUCK
X

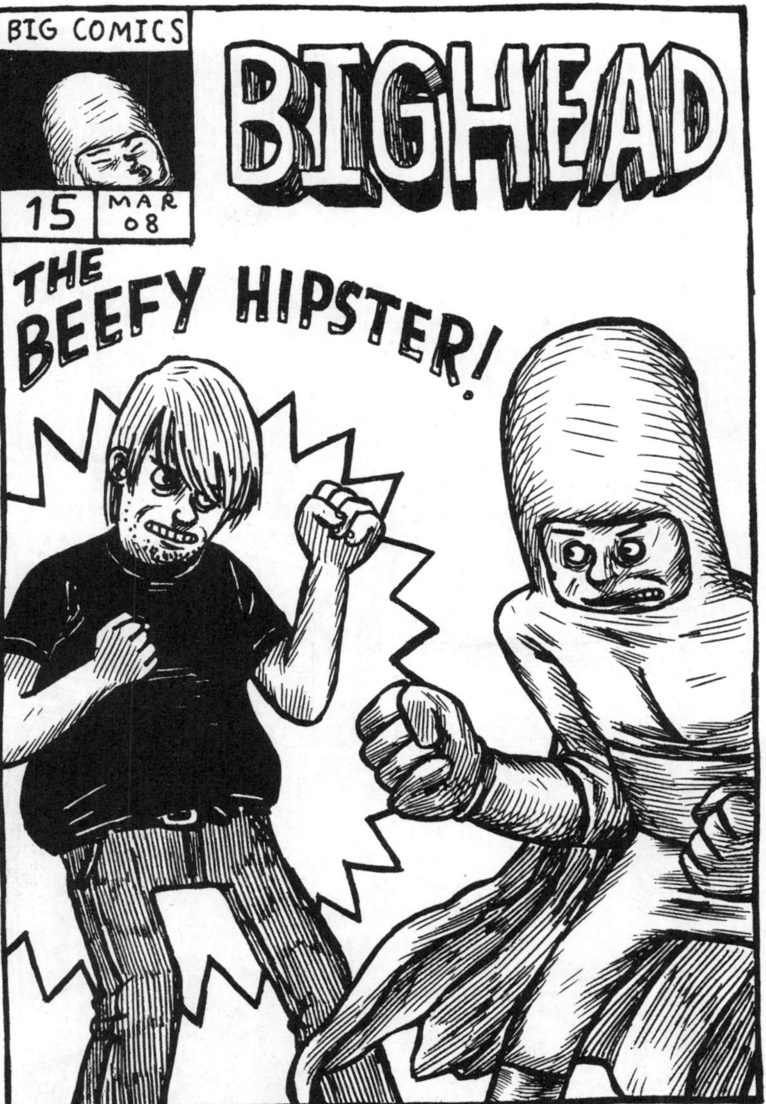
BIG COMICS
BIGHEAD
15
MAR 08
THE BEEFY HIPSTER!

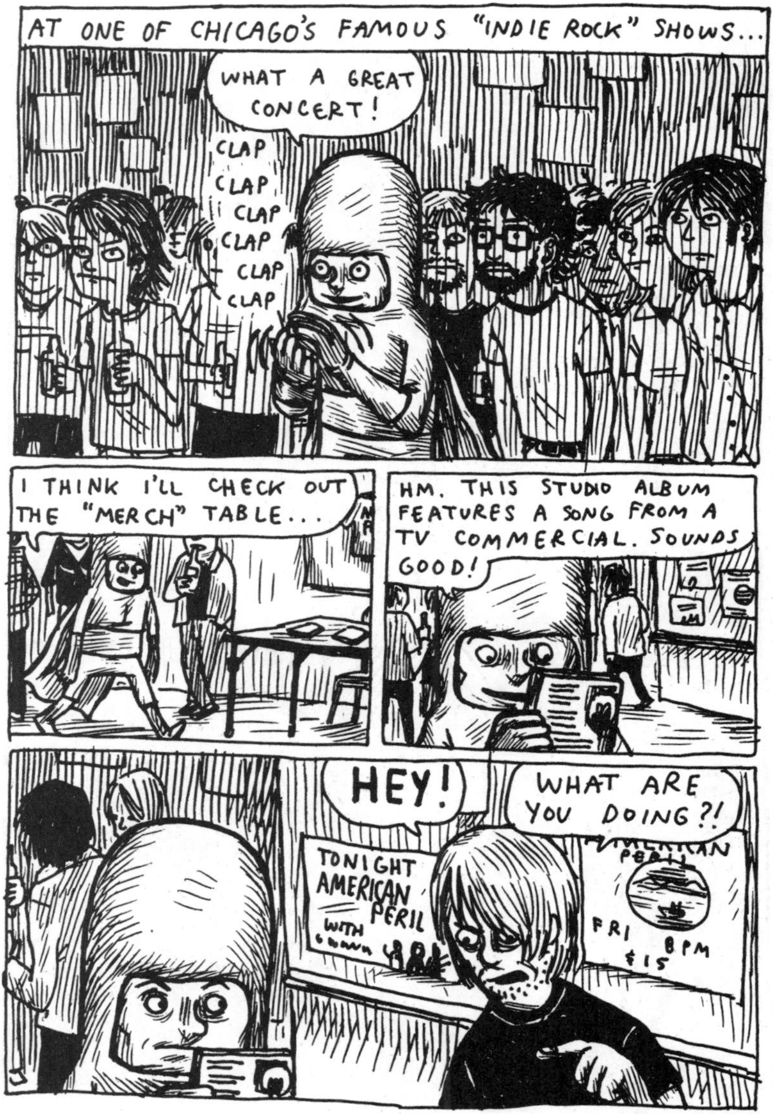
AT ONE OF CHICAGO'S FAMOUS "INDIE ROCK" SHOWS...
WHAT A GREAT CONCERT!
CLAP CLAP CLAP CLAP CLAP CLAP
I THINK I'LL CHECK OUT THE "MERCH" TABLE...
HM. THIS STUDIO ALBUM FEATURES A SONG FROM A TV COMMERCIAL. SOUNDS GOOD!
HEY!
WHAT ARE YOU DOING?!
TONIGHT AMERICAN PERIL WITH
FRI 8PM $15

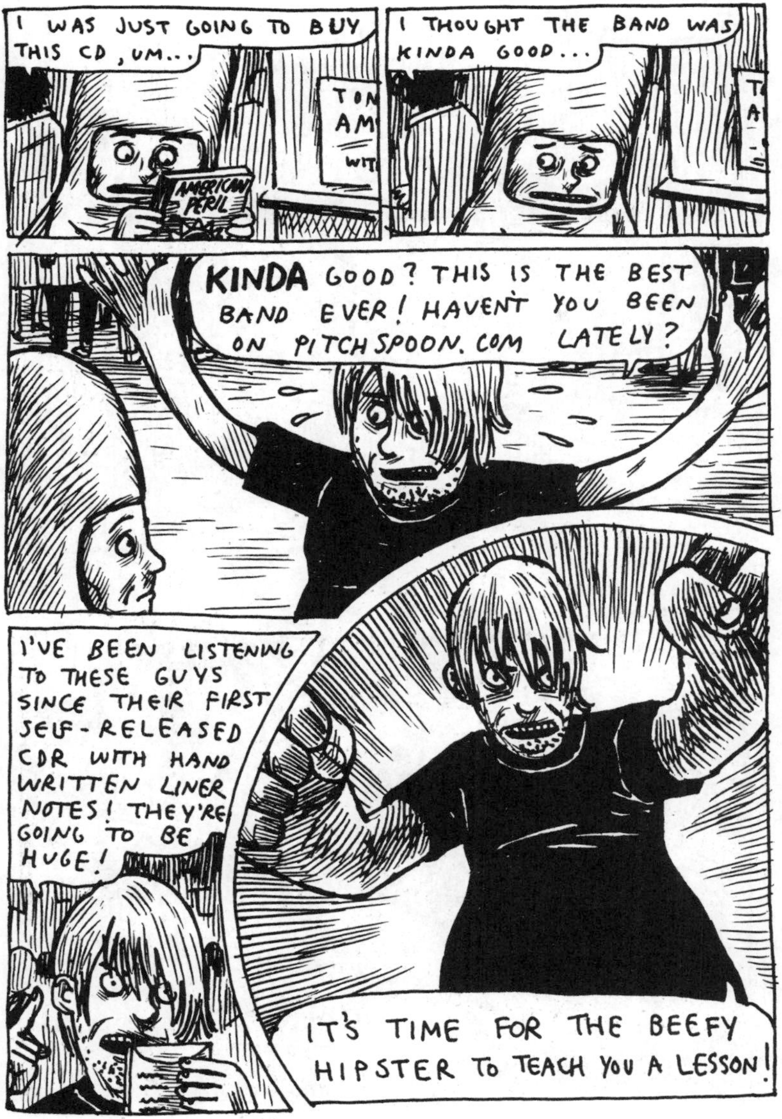
I WAS JUST GOING TO BUY THIS CD, UM...
AMERICAN PERIL
I THOUGHT THE BAND WAS KINDA GOOD...
KINDA GOOD? THIS IS THE BEST BAND EVER! HAVEN'T YOU BEEN ON PITCHSPOON.COM LATELY?
I'VE BEEN LISTENING TO THESE GUYS SINCE THEIR FIRST SELF-RELEASED CDR WITH HAND WRITTEN LINER NOTES! THEY'RE GOING TO BE HUGE!
IT'S TIME FOR THE BEEFY HIPSTER TO TEACH YOU A LESSON!

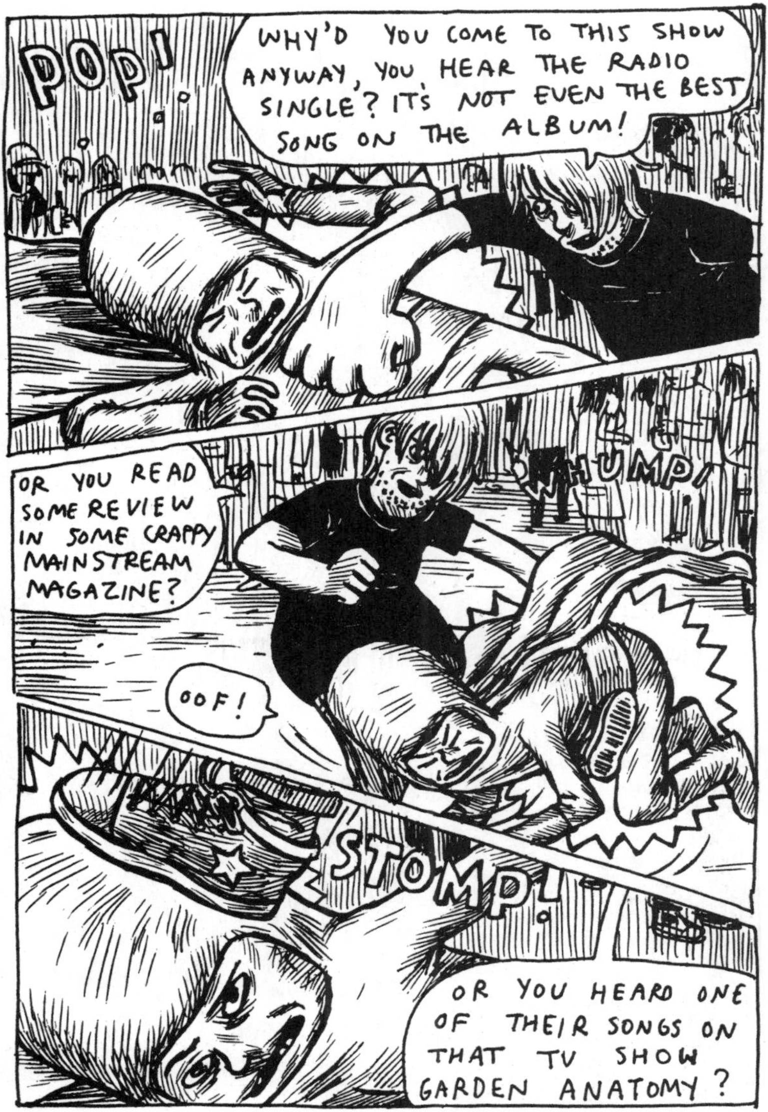
POP!
WHY'D YOU COME TO THIS SHOW ANYWAY, YOU HEAR THE RADIO SINGLE? IT'S NOT EVEN THE BEST SONG ON THE ALBUM!
OR YOU READ SOME REVIEW IN SOME CRAPPY MAINSTREAM MAGAZINE?
HUMP!
OOF!
STOMP!
OR YOU HEARD ONE OF THEIR SONGS ON THAT TV SHOW GARDEN ANATOMY?

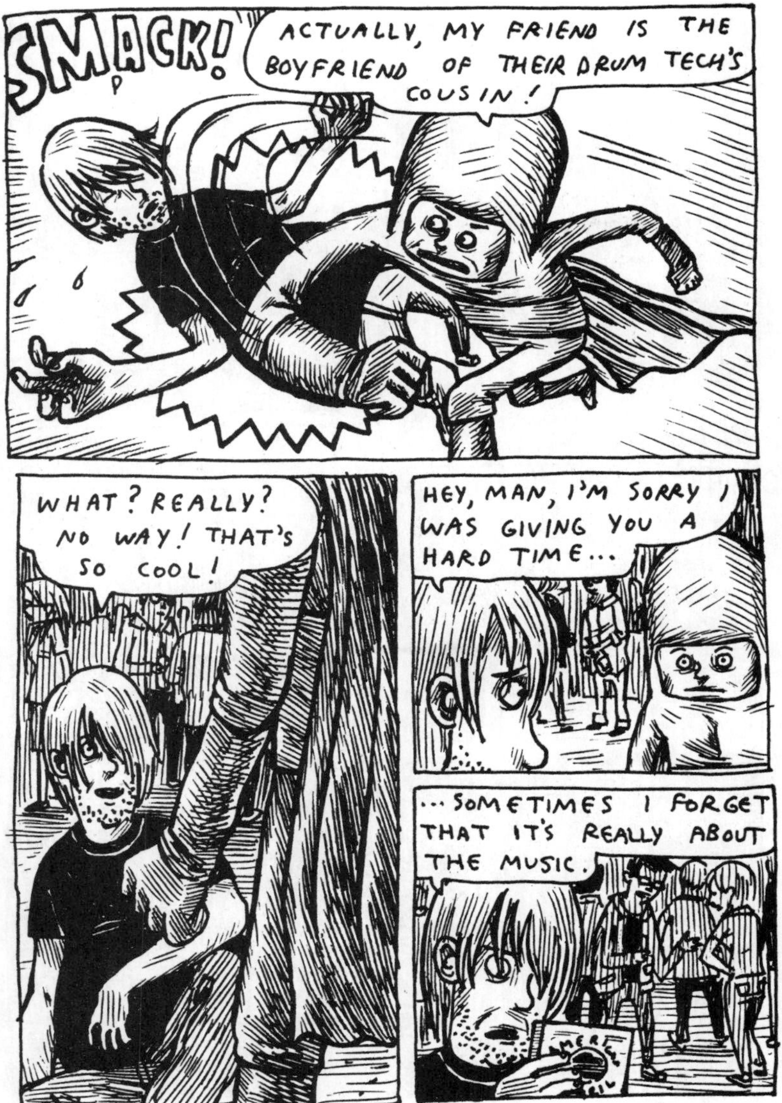
SMACK!
ACTUALLY, MY FRIEND IS THE BOYFRIEND OF THEIR DRUM TECH'S COUSIN!
WHAT? REALLY? NO WAY! THAT'S SO COOL!
HEY, MAN, I'M SORRY I WAS GIVING YOU A HARD TIME...
...SOMETIMES I FORGET THAT IT'S REALLY ABOUT THE MUSIC.

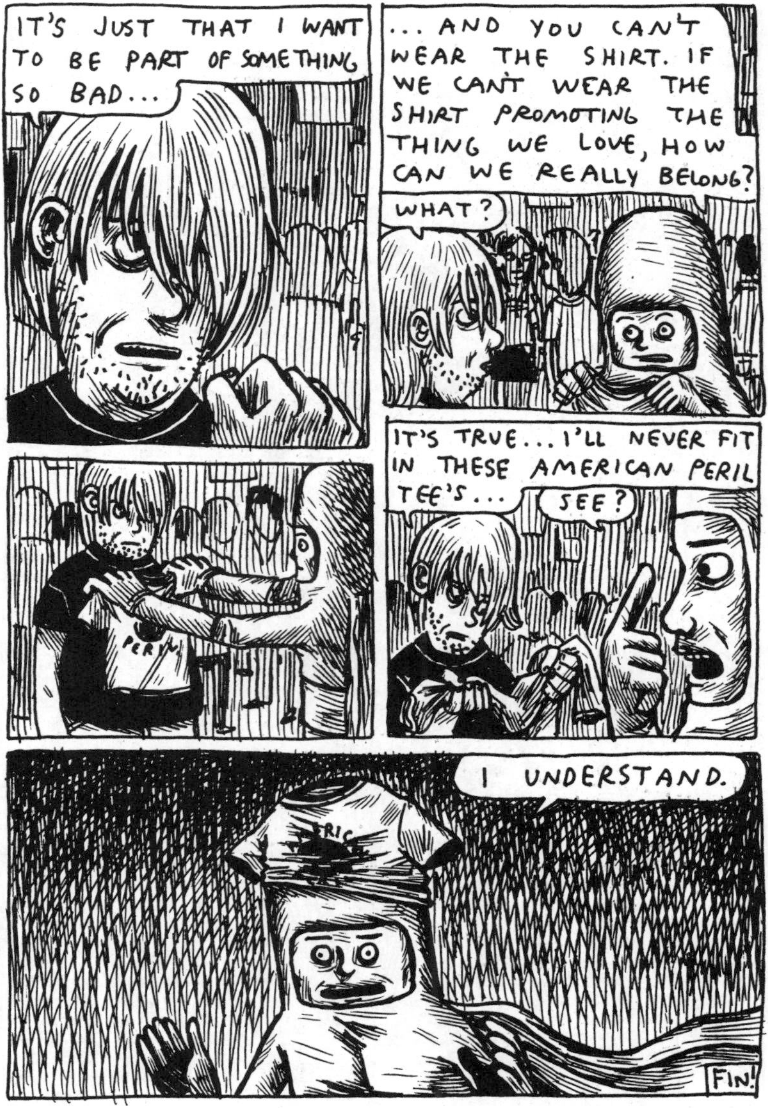
IT'S JUST THAT I WANT TO BE PART OF SOMETHING SO BAD...
... AND YOU CAN'T WEAR THE SHIRT. IF WE CAN'T WEAR THE SHIRT PROMOTING THE THING WE LOVE, HOW CAN WE REALLY BELONG?
WHAT?
PERIL
IT'S TRUE... I'LL NEVER FIT IN THESE AMERICAN PERIL TEE'S...
SEE?
I UNDERSTAND.
FIN!

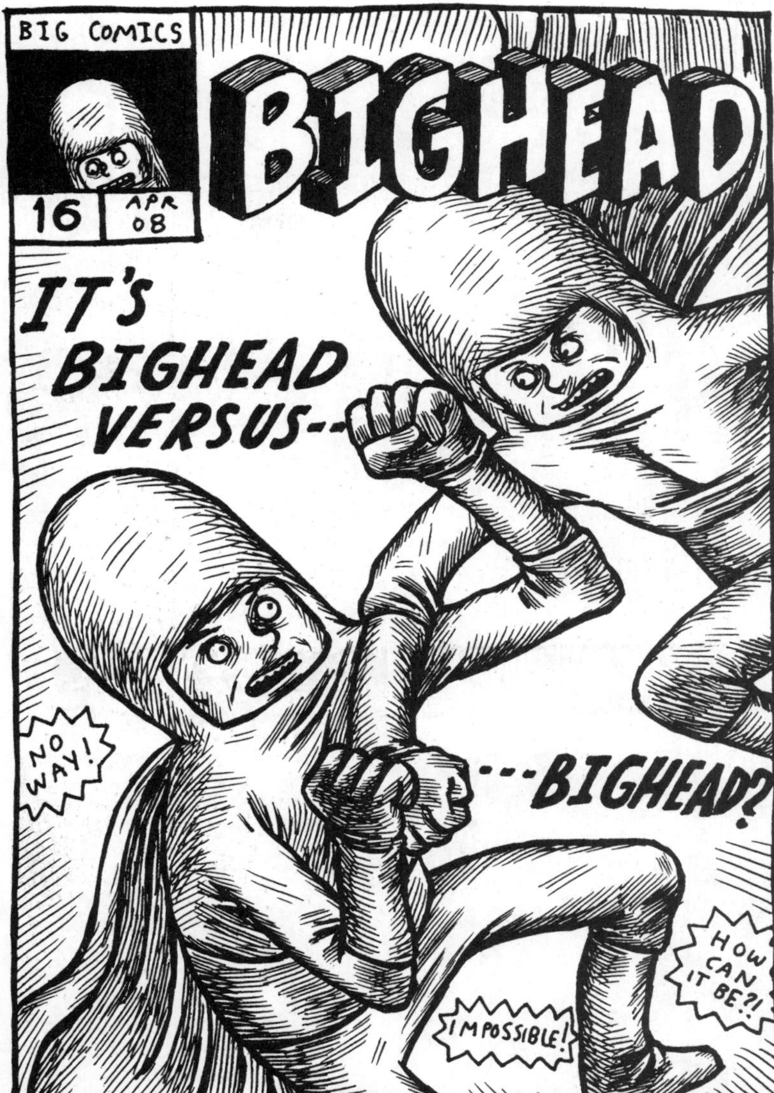
BIG COMICS
BIGHEAD
16
APR 08
IT'S BIGHEAD VERSUS---
---BIGHEAD?
NO WAY!
HOW CAN IT BE?!
IMPOSSIBLE!

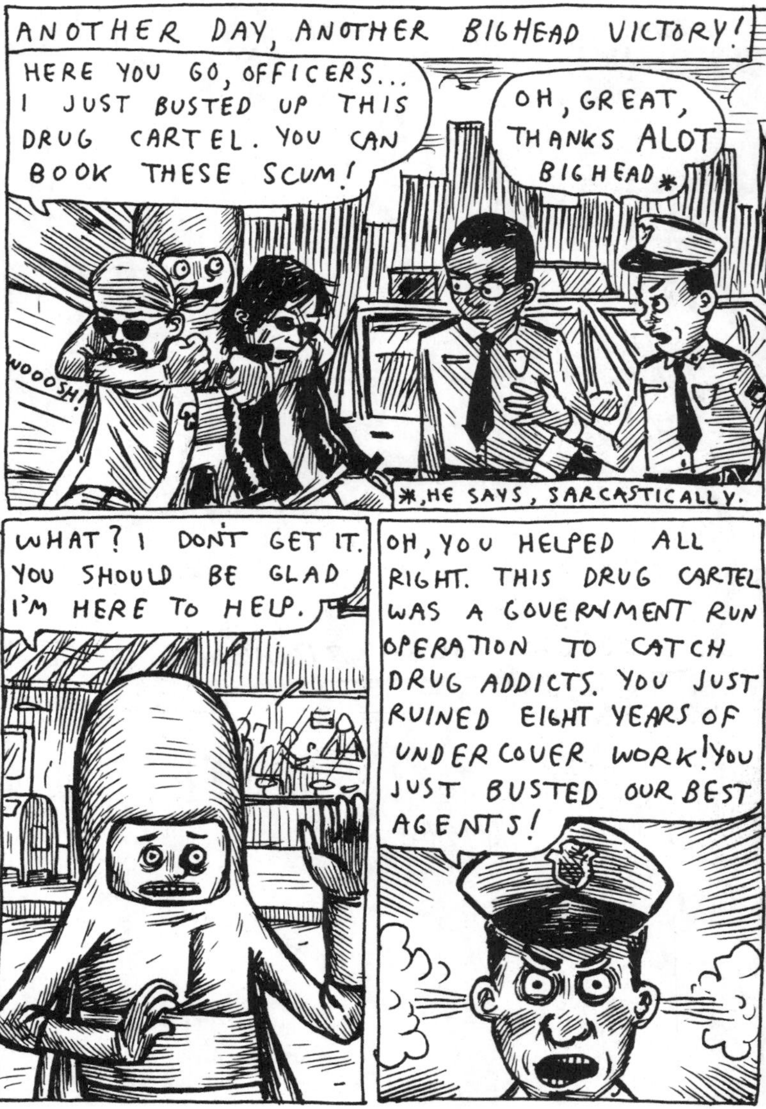
ANOTHER DAY, ANOTHER BIGHEAD VICTORY!
HERE YOU GO, OFFICERS... I JUST BUSTED UP THIS DRUG CARTEL. YOU CAN BOOK THESE SCUM!
OH, GREAT, THANKS ALOT BIGHEAD*
WOOOSH!
*, HE SAYS, SARCASTICALLY.
WHAT? I DON'T GET IT. YOU SHOULD BE GLAD I'M HERE TO HELP.
OH, YOU HELPED ALL RIGHT. THIS DRUG CARTEL WAS A GOVERNMENT RUN OPERATION TO CATCH DRUG ADDICTS. YOU JUST RUINED EIGHT YEARS OF UNDERCOVER WORK! YOU JUST BUSTED OUR BEST AGENTS!

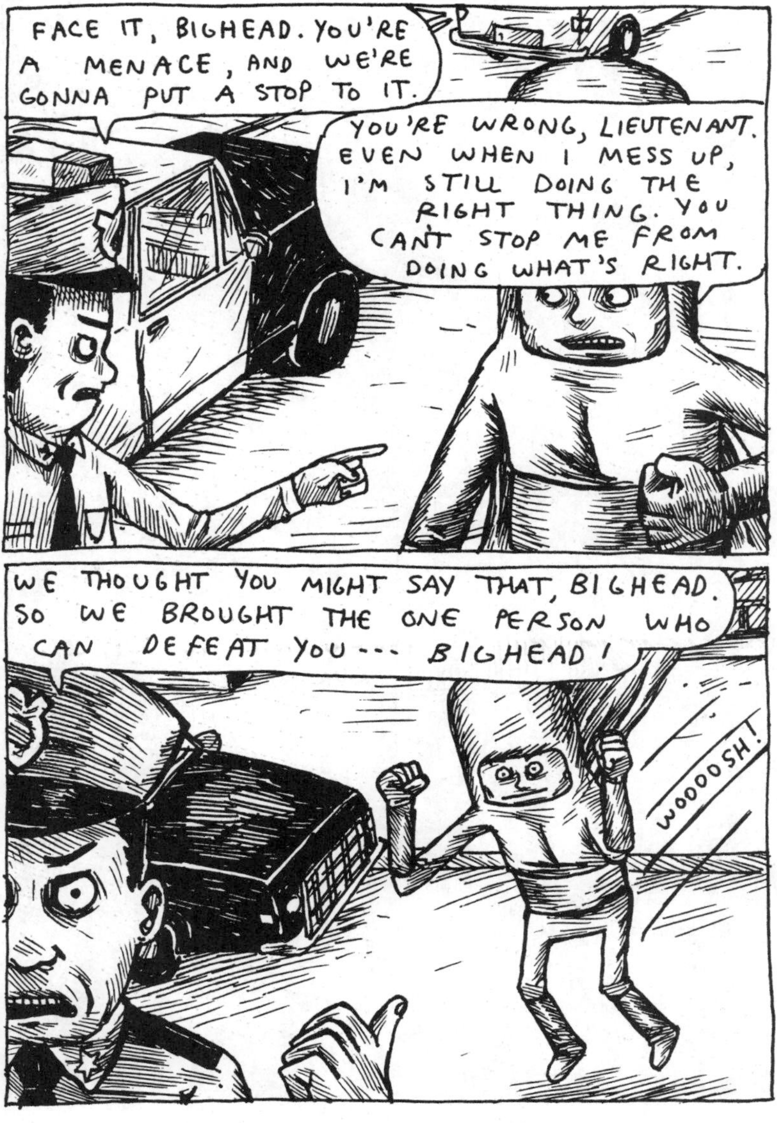
FACE IT, BIGHEAD. YOU'RE A MENACE, AND WE'RE GONNA PUT A STOP TO IT.
YOU'RE WRONG, LIEUTENANT. EVEN WHEN I MESS UP, I'M STILL DOING THE RIGHT THING. YOU CAN'T STOP ME FROM DOING WHAT'S RIGHT.
WE THOUGHT YOU MIGHT SAY THAT, BIGHEAD. SO WE BROUGHT THE ONE PERSON WHO CAN DEFEAT YOU--- BIGHEAD!
WOOOOSH!

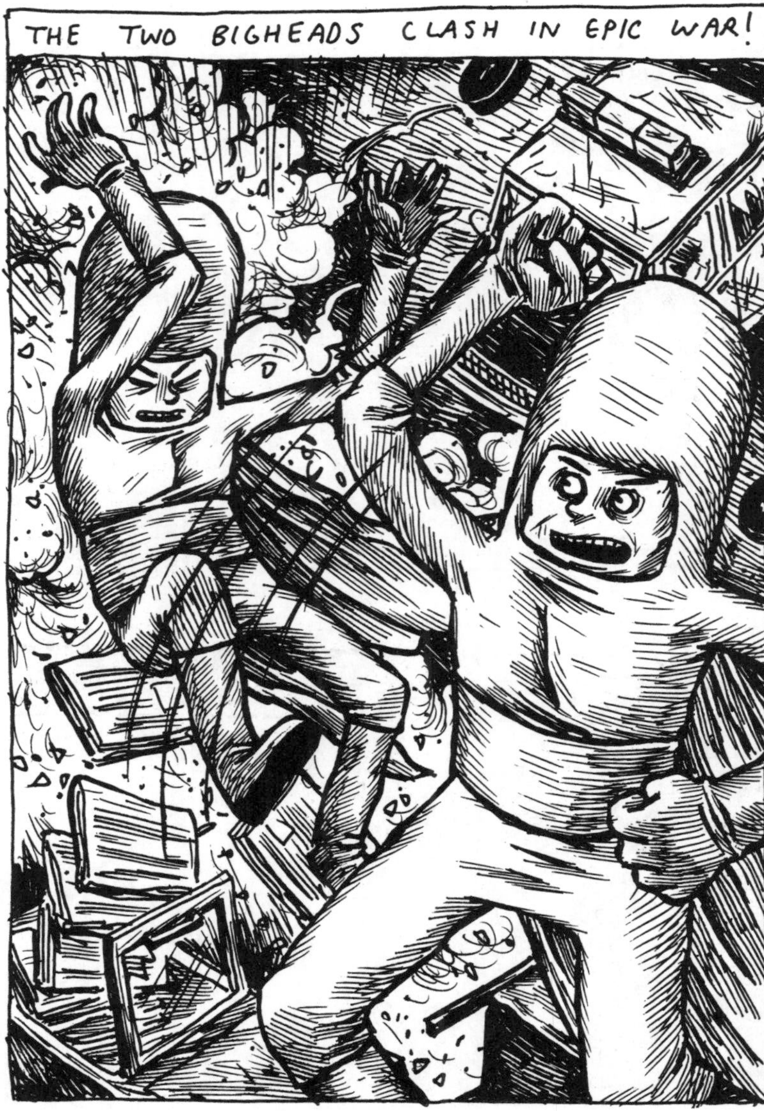
THE TWO BIGHEADS CLASH IN EPIC WAR!

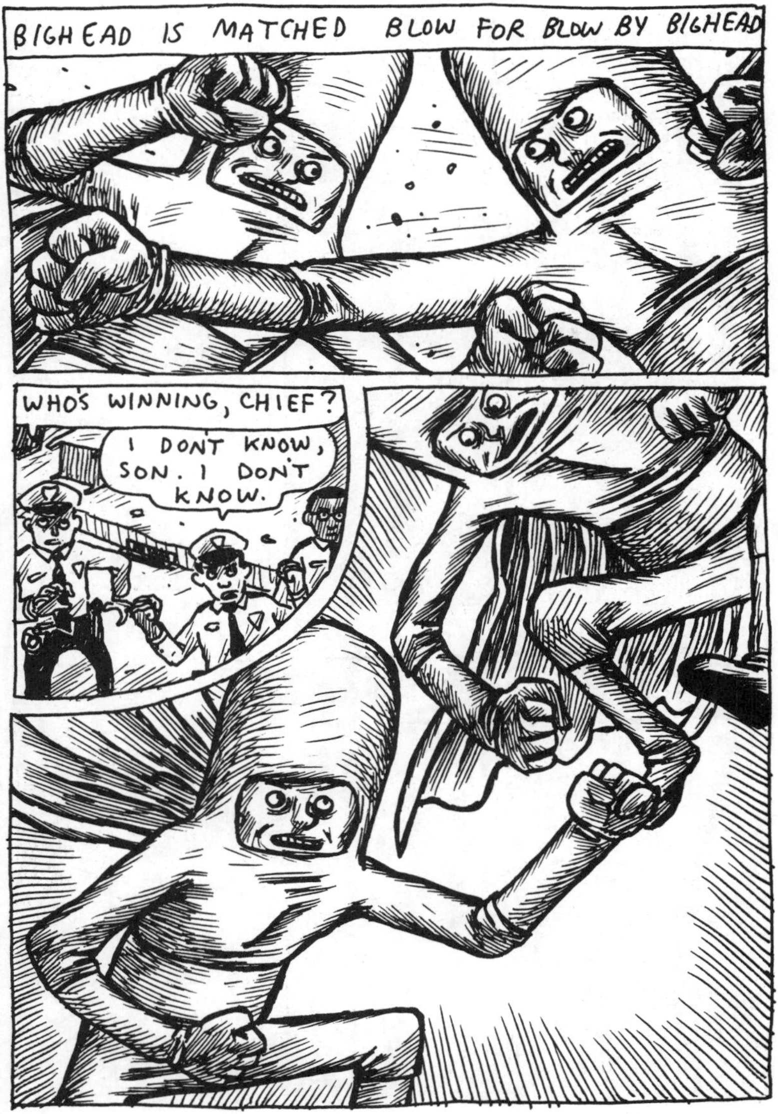
BIGHEAD IS MATCHED BLOW FOR BLOW BY BIGHEAD
WHO'S WINNING, CHIEF?
I DON'T KNOW, SON. I DON'T KNOW.

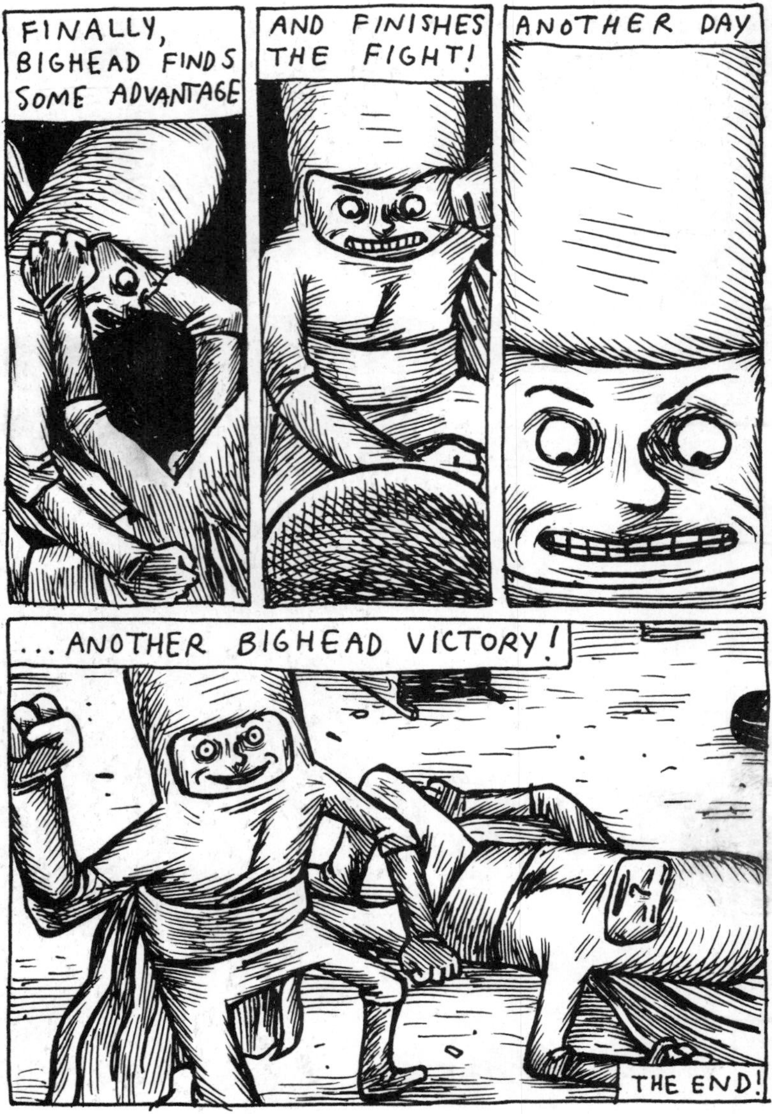
FINALLY, BIGHEAD FINDS SOME ADVANTAGE
AND FINISHES THE FIGHT!
ANOTHER DAY
...ANOTHER BIGHEAD VICTORY!
THE END!